Build a Security Culture

Kai Roer

Build a Security Culture

KAI ROER

IT Governance Publishing

Every possible effort has been made to ensure that the information contained in this book is accurate at the time of going to press, and the publisher and the author cannot accept responsibility for any errors or omissions, however caused. Any opinions expressed in this book are those of the author, not the publisher. Websites identified are for reference only, not endorsement, and any website visits are at the reader's own risk. No responsibility for loss or damage occasioned to any person acting, or refraining from action, as a result of the material in this publication can be accepted by the publisher or the author.

Apart from any fair dealing for the purposes of research or private study, or criticism or review, as permitted under the Copyright, Designs and Patents Act 1988, this publication may only be reproduced, stored or transmitted, in any form, or by any means, with the prior permission in writing of the publisher or, in the case of reprographic reproduction, in accordance with the terms of licences issued by the Copyright Licensing Agency. Enquiries concerning reproduction outside those terms should be sent to the publisher at the following address:

IT Governance Publishing
IT Governance Limited
Unit 3, Clive Court
Bartholomew's Walk
Cambridgeshire Business Park
Ely, Cambridgeshire
CB7 4EA
United Kingdom
www.itgovernance.co.uk

The authors have asserted the rights of the author under the Copyright, Designs and Patents Act, 1988, to be identified as the author of this work.

First published in the United Kingdom in 2015
by IT Governance Publishing

ISBN 978-1-84928-716-6

ACKNOWLEDGEMENTS

This book is the direct result of my engagement and development of the Security Culture Framework. All the people who have been involved in the development and use of the framework are my inspiration to write this book.

The Security Culture Framework is something that evolved in my mind after many years of watching security awareness training programmes being run seemingly without control, metrics and proper planning. Discussing the topic with Lars Haug, we quickly came up with the concept of a holistic framework to help build and maintain security culture. The framework gained interest in both the USA and Europe, within both the public and private sectors. Financial institutions, universities and many others use the framework today.

Roar Thon, at the Norwegian National Security Agency, is one of the very few experts on security culture. His input, questions and support are always helpful, and his generosity is out of this world. Mo Amin, a London-based security consultant, dedicated many hours of his precious time to review the manuscript and concept for the book. Amin is also a key resource on the Security Culture Framework community, and an inspiration to follow. My thanks also to Wolfgang Goerlich for his helpful comments and feedback during the review process.

A special note to Michael Santarcangelo, who provided deep insights through his questions and ideas. I thank you, sir!

Acknowledgements

Numerous discussions about security awareness and culture with fine folks such as Javvad Malik, Thom Langford, Quentyn Taylor, Trond Sundby, Rune Ask, Troy Hunt, Joshua Corman, Per Thorsheim and Brian Honan helped me gain an understanding of what security culture is, and how to best bring it about. We may not always agree, but we certainly do learn!

This book would never have been were it not for Joe Pettit at Informationsecurity Buzz. His introductions and continued support has been vital. Vicki Utting at IT Governance has been a great asset when I tore my hair out over writing this book.

To the information security community worldwide: thank you for keeping me on the edge, for challenging my assumptions and for keeping me safe!

Most importantly, thank you to my dear wife, Karolina, and Leo, my son. You are the light.

ABOUT THE AUTHOR

Kai Roer is a management and security consultant and trainer with extensive international experience from more than 30 countries around the world. He is a guest lecturer at several universities, and the founder of The Roer Group, a European management consulting group focusing on security culture.

Kai has authored a number of books on leadership and cybersecurity, and has been published extensively in print and online, and has appeared on radio, television and featured in printed media. He is a columnist at Help Net Security and is the Cloud Security Alliance Norway Chapter President since 2012.

Kai is a passionate public speaker who engages his audience with his entertaining style and deep topic knowledge of human behaviours, psychology and cybersecurity. He is a Fellow of the National Cybersecurity Institute and runs a blog on information security and culture (roer.com). Kai is the host of Security Culture TV, a monthly video and podcast.

FOREWORD

"May you live in interesting times" is an old saying and one that is certainly applicable to cyber security today. As the unfolding events of the past few years have shown us, we are indeed living in interesting cyber times. The evolving cyber breaches of every sector, be it retail, government, education, financial or others, have been the main focus of the technology conversation this entire year. Big box retailers have been hacked, sensitive data at banks breached, and nation states stand ready to wage cyber warfare.

We have developed computers and the Internet and attached many of the most important aspects of our lives to it. Now we find those connections are at risk due to the activities of 'bad actors' bent on malicious activity. We try to defend our digital systems with properly configured soft and hardware, but in the end it is often a 'people' problem that permits a large portion of the breaches we read about. People are just not following appropriate procedures thereby allowing improper access to systems. As many are aware, the best way to reduce human errors we encounter is through effective education and training. Sadly such education and training around the globe is spotty at best and often wholly inadequate.

With this book, Kai Roer has taken his many years of cyber experience and provided those with a vested interest in cyber security a firm basis on which to build an effective cyber security training programme. This requires change, and understanding how the culture of an organisation needs to change to be effective is vital for cyber success. Each chapter is filled with valuable insights, examples and intuitive thoughts based on his experiences that can easily be transferred to the workplace. As system administrators scramble to harden their respective defences, this work couldn't have come at a better time. Anyone obtaining this book will find it a valuable and informative read.

Dr. Jane LeClair
Chief Operating Officer
National Cybersecurity Institute, Washington, D.C.

CONTENTS

Introduction **1**

    Culture: Does it have to be so hard? 1

Chapter 1: What is Security Culture? **5**

Chapter 2: The Elements of Security Culture **21**

Chapter 3: How Does Security Culture Relate to Security Awareness? **27**

    Attention 36

    Retention 36

    Reproduction 37

    Motivation 37

Chapter 4: Asking for Help Raises Your Chances of Success **41**

Chapter 5: The Psychology of Groups, and How to Use it to Your Benefit **55**

Chapter 6: Measuring Culture **69**

Chapter 7: Building Security Culture **79**

    Metrics 82

    Using SMART goals 84

    The organisation part 85

    Topics 89

    Planner 93

    Setting up your organisation to use the Security Culture Framework 96

Chapter 8: Time is on Your Side **101**

ITG Resources **105**

INTRODUCTION

Culture: Does it have to be so hard?

In this book, I look at organisational culture with information security glasses. In my years of working in the information security industry, I have come across a number of challenges: technical, compliance, and increasingly awareness and security behaviour. Through my travels and company activities, I have learned that a lot of security behaviour challenges are universal: preparing information security information in such a way that it resonates and makes sense for non-security people is a challenge no matter which country or organisation you work in.

I have also learned that some organisations are better at creating the security behaviour they want. Looking at what they do differently, I found that they approach the work with security awareness as a process. They also respect that security competence is exactly that – a competence that must be learned, not just something you tell.

From more than two decades of professional training and consulting in more than 30 different countries, I have also come to learn that if we want people to learn, we need to facilitate learning together with them. Lecturing alone is not creating results. Reading alone makes for very little change. The saying of the Association for Talent Development (ATD[1]) that "Telling ain't Training" is very true. It took me some time to realise that I too had to learn

---

[1] Formerly the American Society for Training and Development (ASTD).

how to train people properly, a realisation that took me on a rollercoaster of learning, exploration and self-development, leading me to develop my training and communication skills across both language barriers and cultural barriers.

The most important thing I learned in these years was to be humble. Humble about my own perspectives – I may think I am right, and I may have all the experience to tell me I am right, but implant me in Tunisia or Japan and most of my perspectives and experience in treating and communicating with people no longer hold. I learned this the hard way, leading me to realise that there are more ways of doing things than I first accounted for, and that others may achieve great success by choosing a different path than the one I chose.

The same is true with organisational culture. There are many ways of building, changing and maintaining organisational culture. It is one of those areas where scientists and practitioners still argue about the right approach[2]. My experience is that the right approach depends on each case. Every organisation is unique and comes with its own culture and subcultures. Some are great, some really poor. All of them impact the behaviour, ideas and thoughts of the employees. The question becomes: how do we take control of that culture?

---

[2] A quick search through academic papers via Google will amply demonstrate the variety of approaches within academia alone, while a similar review of the titles available on Amazon reveals a similar breadth among practitioners. For a comprehensive review of the topic (and many other topics!), read Bernard Bass' *The Bass Handbook of Leadership: Theory, Research, and Managerial Applications.*

As luck has it, there are processes and methods to apply when you want to build and manage culture. Instead of trying to come up with everything yourself, you can learn from frameworks like the Security Culture Framework[3]. Using a framework gives you a clear path with checkpoints and actions that ensure your efforts are moving in the right direction. This is not to say that changing culture is easy, nor fast: it may require many small steps iterated over time. Using a structured approach helps you to do the right things at the right time, making success more likely.

The book consists of eight chapters, each looking at a different aspect of security culture. Chapter one introduces the concept of security culture, provides a definition and sets the stage. In chapter two, I look at the three building bricks of culture: technology, policy and people. I also bind the three together and show how they impact one another.

In chapter three, I look at how security culture relates to security awareness, and I will show how awareness is only one of the elements that is required to change behaviour and culture. Next, in chapter four, I explain why we as security professionals are not the people who should build culture – at least not alone – and who you should involve in your organisation. In chapter five, I point to social psychology and research on how we interact with other people. You will also learn how you can use the knowledge of how groups impact our lives to increase your chances of improving security culture.

---

[3] The Security Culture Framework describes a structured approach to developing an effective and consistent security culture within an organisation. Read more about it here: *https://scf.roer.com*.

In chapter six, I make the case for why we need to measure our security culture efforts, and point to some ways to do just that. Finally, in *chapter 7*, I introduce the Security Culture Framework, and walk you through how it is built. This chapter also includes some templates you can use in your own security culture programmes.

Depending on your perspective, I may provide new insights and ideas on how to build security culture. I hope I can inspire you to take a structured approach to building and maintaining good security culture. Even if you do choose a structured approach, you will experience that it takes time to get the results you want. Small steps, iterated over time, is the key. Knowing where you are, and where you want to be, is vital, and one of the key elements in a structured approach.

CHAPTER 1: WHAT IS SECURITY CULTURE?

An introduction to the topic, with an introduction to the definition of culture (based on sociology) and how it relates to security.

Humans are animals who live in groups; we flock. In any group of animals there exists a hierarchy, levels that every animal in the group follows. Each of these levels comes with rules to abide by, including understanding who is above you, who is below you and what your particular level allows you to do.

Consider a wolf pack[4]. They show the hierarchy very clearly, with the Alpha couple on the top, giving them the right to rule as they please. Below them are sergeants, animals in the pack with more power than most and which police the group if necessary. Below the sergeants are normal members, workers if you like, and below these again are one or a few of lesser rights – the one or two wolves that are constantly being picked on. Every animal in the pack has the right to food, shelter, safety and protection – as long as they abide by the rules and accept their level. A wolf on the lower levels will quickly and

---

[4] It should be noted that the traditional view of a wolf pack as led by an Alpha and his mate is a grand simplification, and many biologists prefer to refer to 'breeder wolves' (note the plural) as the centre of the pack. This does not undermine my point here, however, as the broader structure of the pack as a unit offering its members protection and belonging in exchange for acceptance of the rules and hierarchy is undoubted.

effectively be controlled by the other wolves if he or she dares to step out of line.

Even the poorest wolf in the pack is entitled to the pack's protection against external threat. They are also entitled to love and care, even if they are expected to give more than they receive.

The wolves in the pack accept the hierarchy, rules and domestic violence because they receive protection from external threat, they get to eat and they may even enjoy the sense of belonging. It makes sense for the wolves to stick together, even if the price an individual wolf pays is a certain loss of personal freedom.

We see similar tendencies and mechanisms play out in human society. The first rule of living in a society is to accept the rules. To do that, we also need to understand the rules, how they are constituted and how they are playing out.

Consider the wolf pack again. Let us imagine a new wolf is in the pack (it could be a puppy becoming an adult, or adoption, or anything else). This new wolf is entering the pack at the second-to-lowest level, so he is accepted as a worker, someone with little status. However, this particular wolf cannot understand the rules at play, and imagines himself as the leader of the pack. At first, the other wolves just mock him a bit, to remind him of his place. Then, when he clearly does not get the message, they become more violent, with the Alphas and their sergeants leading the punishment. The violence continues until the wolf rolls over on his back and surrenders. He gets the message, he understands that there is someone else above him in the chain of command, and that if he wants to survive and be a part of the pack, he must accept his role, his place.

Just like the wolf, we need a basic understanding of authority if we want to succeed in life.

Thankfully, luck is with us. According to some scientists, the human brain is hardwired to understand the power structure of the people in a room[5], and to automatically identify with our own level. This particular science is based on babies, too young to communicate verbally, who still recognise the power levels and authorities in a room.

Why does this matter to us? This kind of research suggests that the need for policies, rules and laws is part of the basic functioning of the human mind. It suggests that although the way we currently organise our societies can be considered social constructs, we humans (social animals) come pre-programmed with the ability to form, abide by and live in groups based on different levels and authorities.

It basically tells us that our ability to live together in small and large groups is a biologically developed ability. We are meant to form groups and find ways of living together.

This is an important backdrop to understanding what culture is. According to the Oxford English Dictionary, culture is:

> "The ideas, customs and social behaviours of a particular people or group."[6]

---

[5] In the study "Big and Mighty: Preverbal Infants Mentally Represent Social Dominance" (L. Thomsen, W.E. Frankenhuis, M. Ingold-Smith and S. Carey), it was found that babies expect larger individuals to win in a conflict. For a baby to make that prediction, they must have some comprehension that individuals have goals, and that these goals can conflict with other individuals' goals. Furthermore, they must understand that these conflicts have winners and losers.

[6] There are a number of different definitions of culture, including security culture. I have chosen the ones I use in this book based on the premise that they

Part of the behaviours we see in culture can be traced back to basic human biology as I showed earlier. It is good to know that culture is such a base need in us, as it shows the importance of living, working and functioning together.

Most of culture may not be so basic, and it is certainly not traced to biology alone. Most culture is learned[7]. One of my favourite examples is how people walk. "How can the way people walk be culture?" you may ask.

That is a fair question, considering that we all walk the same way. We all put one foot in front of the other. So far, I agree.

What is different is *how* we put one foot in front of the other.

In the western world, where I grew up and lived most of my life, we wear shoes. Mostly comfortable shoes, enabling us to thump our heels onto the ground without being hurt (at least not right away). We also wear high heels, which is not exactly a natural way of walking, even if walking on your toe-balls and mid-foot is considered the natural way of walking.

---

describe what I discuss in layman's terms, which makes it accessible for people outside of academia.

[7] This is also debated – behaviorists take this stand, while naturalists believe behavior (and thus culture) to be inherited, more similarly to genetic inheritance. The truth is likely somewhere between those extremes. Richerson and Boyd describe the naturalists' position: "Cultural variants are more like genes than are ordinary learned variants. Like genes, they are inherited and transmitted in a potentially endless chain, while variants acquired by individual learning are lost with the death of the learner." ("Cultural Inheritence and Evolutionary Ecology", *Evolutionary Ecology and Human Behaviour*, 1992.)

Unconvinced? Come with me to Africa, then. Here, many people walk barefoot, which means they walk differently from you. Go to Kenya, where some tribes run because they consider walking a waste of their time. Am I getting there? Not yet? Well, my last example is from Asia.

In Japan, traditional shoes are made of a plank, with two wooden pieces underneath. Walking with these shoes dictates a particular walking style – instead of lifting your feet, you slide them along the ground, sort of.

Still not following me? Wear high heels one day, and I promise you will get the idea. How we walk is learned behaviour. A behaviour dictated by the culture we live in. Your ability to recognise what I mean by my claim about walking, is cultural: it is a learned behaviour. It depends mostly on your exposure to different cultures, different people and different places.

The definition of culture is the same: *ideas, customs and social behaviour of a particular people or group*

As we have seen in the preceding example, ideas, customs and social behaviour are collections of many things – from how we walk, to how we speak, to how we think and interact. Instead of thinking about culture across borders, let us look closer to where we work. Consider your workplace. Culture is not one thing only; it is the accumulation of many groups of people: the sales department, the accounting department, the IT department, the developers, the builders, testers and so on. Each of these departments has its own more or less distinct culture – ideas, customs and social behaviours that belong to that particular department. Together, these *subcultures* form the company culture. And some of these departments are also subdivided into other subcultures: smokers, the high achievers, the slackers, the coffee drinkers, the problem solvers and so on (I am sure you can think of others more fitting to your organisation).

You, as an individual, are a member of many different groups, and more or less abide by each group's cultural rules. In your workplace, you may be working as a mid-level manager, drinking coffee, placed in the IT division and be a high achiever. Each of these groups comes with a cultural attachment.

Outside your workspace, you also belong to different groups, each with different characteristics: your family, your extended family, perhaps you are a parent, you may be playing sports (each team/group you belong to has different subcultures), you are a community member and so on.

Each of the groups you belong to follows the same basic principles. They consist of People: the members; Policies: the rules this particular group follow, sometimes written and always the unwritten ones; and Technology: the tools, methods and models used by this group. You can read more about these three elements, and how they come together to form and change culture, in *Chapter Two*.

Now that we have a quick introduction to culture, let us examine it from a security perspective.

According to the Oxford dictionary, security can be defined as:

"The state of being free from danger or threat."

Using this definition helps us understand what we as security professionals do: our job is to create an environment where our colleagues can work in a *state of being free from danger and threat;* they can do what they are supposed to, knowing that they will be taken good care of, that external threats and dangers are being kept outside.

In the image of the wolf pack, this becomes very clear: as a member of the pack, each of the wolves are entitled to food, to protection from external threat and to know their place. They get *security* by living in the pack. The same strategy is used by a number of different creatures, and has proved very successful.

One way of being free from danger is to know the social structure, and your own place in it. Understanding where you are in the organisation, and what is expected of you is crucial to properly functioning in a group. This is one of the reasons it is important to communicate clearly, and to express the security behaviour you want in your organisation in a way that employees can relate to.

Since culture and social behaviour is so engraved in us by nature, it makes perfect sense to understand how to use nature's own strategies to enhance security in our organisations. Enter Security Culture.

Think of security culture as one subculture of your organisation's culture. The security culture is the part of your organisation's culture that focuses on security, *to help people into the state of being free from threat or danger*, and you can apply the same techniques used by organisational theorists, transformational theory, sociology and psychology to understand and enhance your organisation's security culture.

Using the two preceding definitions, we can define security culture as

"The ideas, customs and social behaviours of a particular people or group that helps them be free from threat and danger."

Security culture is the ideas, customs and social behaviour that your organisation, and its subgroups, have, use and act upon to create a state of being free from threat and danger.

The way your organisation treats passwords is part of security culture. How your employees detect and act upon a stranger in the building is part of security culture. How you define policies, implement them and train employees in security behaviour all impact your security culture.

In fact, all the social behaviours in your organisation impact your security culture. Security culture also impacts all social behaviour in your organisation: it becomes a question of who is in charge of the social behaviour, You or the Culture.

Sometimes I hear that changing culture is impossible, or at least very hard to do. As with security awareness, who some find very hard to teach successfully, cultural change is possible. It is, in fact, a given. Culture is, according to sociology, plastic[8]. It adapts to its members.

Think of it like this: without a group of people, there would be no culture. Culture demands at least two people.

---

[8] The other characteristics of culture are generally given in the following statements: culture is learned and acquired; culture is shared and transmitted; culture is social; culture is ideational; culture gratifies human needs; culture tends towards integration; and culture is cumulative. (E. Palispis, *Introduction to Sociology and Anthropology*, 2007.)

These two people, together, form the ideas, customs and social behaviour of this particular group, by their actions and activities. The culture is likely highly influenced by the larger culture that formed the two members in the first place – including language, social belief and so on. Even so, the group will form a distinct subculture, with its own rules, ideas and customs.

Then, some time later, the group welcomes a third member. This new member brings her own ideas, customs and social behaviours. Let us say that the group's initial members met at a pub and drank beer once a week. The new member meets them too, but starts drinking wine instead. Just by drinking wine instead of beer, the culture of the group has changed: it can no longer say "we drink only beer." We may even imagine that six months later, the whole group moved from the pub to a restaurant and they are all drinking wine while enjoying fine dining. The group is the same three members, but the culture has changed a lot!

This example shows how quickly, and easily, culture can change if the majority of the members, or the ones with the right authority, set out to do so. It also shows that culture can change *regardless* of original intent. In this particular group, a stranger created enough impact to change the whole group culture.

Another example is the coffee-machine example where someone begins working at a new employer. The new employee is a coffee drinker, and quickly figures out where the coffee machine is. As soon as she knows where it is, she only takes a few days to adapt her behaviour to the coffee culture at the location, no matter how they do their coffee-machine ritual.

This example shows how quickly we as individuals adopt a new culture when we are correctly *incentivised*[9].

The impact of individuals in a group is very important. Think of a group of people, say a team at work. This group has no strong culture, and are a loosely knit team of people working together. Without a strong culture, a group like this is more vulnerable to outside pressure, and to uncontrolled cultural change.

Into this group comes a new team member. This person is very negative. He sees problems everywhere, and is a specialist in killing enthusiasm. Suggesting an idea to this guy is a sure-fire way to be shot down, publicly humiliated and buried under a pile of sarcastic rocks. And no, it does not matter who approaches him with suggestions, ideas and opportunities: he immediately says things like, "No, it's never gonna happen" or "I saw this before, it failed." On particularly bad days, he may even say "Are you stupid, or what?"

What happens to a group when such a person is introduced? It depends on the group's culture. A group with a strong culture is more likely to change the newcomer into conforming with the culture (or force him out), whereas a group with no strong culture is more likely formed by the new member. In this case, since the group has no strong culture, they quickly become a gang of grumps. Their production rate deteriorates, and their

---

[9] According to motivational theory, there are two broad forms of incentive: intrinsic and extrinsic. An intrinsic incentive is derived internally – the individual is motivated to perform because they enjoy the work or the challenge, for instance. An extrinsic motivation is applied from without – the employer offers a cash bonus if the employee completes a task quickly, for instance. It should be noted that there are negative forms of both types of incentive, such as the threat of being fired, etc.

problem solving is replaced with problem focus: instead of finding solutions, they only see problems. The group adopts the newcomer's attitude.

In this example, a productive and functioning team was destroyed by just one person. Imagine the cost for the organisation that this cultural change has. Then consider the personal and interpersonal costs involved in this cultural change: people in the group are no longer happy to go to work, and they may even change their social behaviour towards their friends and families!

That is the kind of impact culture has on people, and the impact people have on culture. Since I *choose* to be a positive force wherever I go, I will end this chapter on a positive note.

Consider the same group as before, a team of people working together. There is no strong culture in the group, and their social behaviours, as before, are neutral and flexible. This time, the team member we introduce is a positive person, one who sees opportunities where others see problems, and one who helps people succeed instead of killing every idea.

Since the culture in the group is neutral, our new group member can easily change it, just like we saw with the negative example before. Just like the negative influencer, positivity is contagious too. At first, one or two of the other team members will enforce their positive traits, and after some time, the positivity spreads throughout the whole team.

Other teams in the organisation will notice too, and may want to join the team – after all, who does not want to be a part of a success?

These examples show us how culture can be a vulnerability to your organisation too. When it comes to changing culture, going from a neutral, weak culture is easy. To change a strong culture may not be so simple. Understanding the cultural impact on your organisation, and to your security programme, is vital if you want to create a human stronghold to fence off external threat.

In the next chapter we will look at the building blocks of human culture: People/Competence, Policies and Technology.

Case Study: Introducing John, chief information security officer

A case for Culture

John is a chief information security officer (CISO) in a large bank. He is, as most CISOs are, a very busy man, juggling strategic planning with tactic reporting, and trying to make his team of three do every task they need to, while also securing budgets to improve security around the bank.

For a long time, John has tried to train the employees on awareness. To ensure compliance, he runs security awareness training for all new hires, a part of the bank's employee on-boarding programme. He also has at least one awareness training campaign running throughout the bank every year. In his reports to the directors, he states that 95% of new hires have

---

successfully completed the on-boarding training programme, and he also reports an 87% open rate and a 64% completion rate of the annual awareness programme.

John is not confident that his reports are meaningful, and he is not sure if the numbers are showing the bank's actual awareness level. In fact, John is uncertain if his ongoing efforts are creating any results at all, as successful phishing attempts have risen during the past 12 months, and a steadily growing number of password reset requests is a concern. In addition, he has a hard time motivating any of his team members to do any awareness work at all, even when he gives them direct orders.

In a recent board meeting, where he presented his numbers on awareness, Jillian, one of the directors, asked him if the numbers meant that the bank was in a secure state, and she also wanted to know how their bank compares to other banks in the industry.

Puzzled by Jillian's questions, he said he was confident in his numbers, and that as far as he knew they were doing ok. Only after the meeting did he realise that he did not really know. He decided to look into the matter.

Over the next month, John spent his time researching. What he found was alarming. The more he looked at his numbers, the more he realised they were vanity metrics – a term coined by Eric Ries in his book *The Lean Startup*, a book John was told by one of his friends to read. Vanity metrics are numbers that looks good, and seemingly provide value, but in reality do not provide any answers. John realised that his reports for the past few years did not give him or his bank any real measurement of their progress, nor the reality of their security culture and behaviours.

He also realised there were very few benchmarks on security awareness, and that he had no clue whether or not his bank was as good as the others.

As part of his research, John also stumbled upon the Security Culture Framework. He approached me, and together we created a three-year plan to change the approach of his security awareness efforts: we created a plan to build security culture. We devised a plan for John to create a metric that allowed him to understand his landscape. We also defined a series of goals, which he described in a way that ensured he would know when he hit, or by how far he missed, his targets.

Another challenge that surfaced in our talks was the lack of strategic cooperation between the security team and the rest of the organisation. John and his team would do their configurations, implement policies, put out fires and so on, and most of their communications with other departments were perceived by the organisation as being negative. Many saw John and his team as naysayers. Using the organisation module, John learned to adapt a few strategic communication tools, and to build rapport with people and managers around the bank. I also urged him to build a deep and meaningful relationship with Human Resources.

Finally, John needed a way to handle his team's negativity towards awareness work. When asked, a team member would reluctantly accept an awareness-related task, but it was very clear that none of the team members found that kind of work interesting. John had to tackle this challenge, and quickly!

Throughout this book we will follow John as he endeavours to build security culture, by digging into each of the preceding cases.

CHAPTER 2: THE ELEMENTS OF SECURITY CULTURE

We will look at the elements that together make security culture: technology, policies/rules and people/competence, and how they work together to form culture.

Social behaviour, ideas and customs are to a large degree based upon rules. Some rules are written into laws, regulations and standards. Other rules, most of them in fact, are unwritten and come in the form of ethics, moral codes and our mutual ideas of what is acceptable behaviour in the different groups we belong to.

In this chapter I refer to all rules, laws, regulations, ethics, moral codes and so on as *policies*. To make it absolutely clear: policies in this context is more than just written policies in your organisation. In this context, policies comprise the written *and* unwritten rules that regulate our ideas, customs and social behaviours.

Technology is also a wide area. From the Mars Rover, to your phone and car, to the glasses some people use to help see – these are all technology. In this context, I will use the word *technology* to describe any tool – made or not – that we use in a determined way. A rock you use to crack open a coconut is considered technology by this definition. A club our forefathers used to go hunting, to protect themselves or to look cool is a tool. The bow and arrow is a tool.

Evidently, technology is a wide area, one that goes back to the origins of man. Interestingly, man is not the only one who uses tools to a means. Some birds use sticks, at least one type of octopus uses tools to get food and different kinds of apes use rocks to crack open nuts.

Technology is not only about tangible things like computers, cars, hammers and so on, but also models: mental models (patterns and schemas in our mind) as well as patterns, standards and models used as templates and starting points.

The third part of the triangle is *people*. It is people who use the technology, and it is people who form and inform the policies. The society you are brought up in determines your policies and your use of tools. As described in *Chapter 1*, social behaviour is learned behaviour. We can think of culture as *competence*, the knowledge and understanding of how to function properly in a social group. This competence includes how to use technology, and at least the basic rules of engagement in our society.

These three elements – People, Policies and Technology – give us perspectives to the world. The more we understand their formation and their continued interaction, the easier it is to understand how we can use them to build and maintain security culture.

Each of these elements directly impacts the other two. No matter where the change happens, the other two elements are changed too.

Imagine Thor. He lived in long-forgotten times, back when phones and cars and even horseback riding were unheard of. Thor learned from his mother that he could use a rock to crack open nuts. One day, Thor saw a small deer nearby and threw a rock at it. It was a lucky hit, and the deer fell to the ground, to the amazement of Thor's tribe. Soon after, every member of the tribe started experimenting with throwing rocks, sticks and so on at animals.

Thor took a known technology, the rock, and repurposed it to do something new. In modern language we call this innovation. Back then, they were just happy to eat fresh meat.

This example shows us how people can use technology, and through their use, create new opportunities. It is similar to what Apple did with the iPod: MP3 players already let you store your whole collection of CDs on the device, but what did not exist was a commercially viable ecosystem for the sale and distribution of electronic music – from artists to consumer in one easy step.

Another example is the development of firewalls from its initial start as a port master, into highly advanced filtering devices capable of looking for malicious content during transit.

Let us go back to Thor.

As the use of throwing rocks grew, another tribal member threw a large rock at a fellow tribe member, killing him. The rock had changed from nut cracker, to a hunting tool, and finally a murder weapon.

At this point, the tribe had to consider the use of the rock. Some folks advocated the need to only accept the rock as a nut cracker, whereas the hunters argued strongly that the need for fresh meat meant they should be allowed to continue using the rock too. After many talks, discussion and debate, the tribe finally agreed that rocks, and any similar tools, were only allowed to be used as intended, in this case crushing nuts and hunting food, but not to kill people.

Everyone rejoiced and the party lasted for many days.

For the tribe, and for mankind, this was one of the first formal policies adopted. The policy was created based on how people used the technology: the policy was initiated by technology. Throughout history we see the same scenario: a technological innovation enables both positive (hunting for food) and negative (killing tribe members) possibilities. As we learn of the consequences, we adapt our social behaviour, customs and ideas and form policies. Some are written, and some are not.

You can of course substitute Thor's rock with any other tool ever used by mankind. The point remains the same: the use of tools is regulated by our ideas, customs and social behaviours, which are strongly informed by policies.

Just as technology creates policies, policies can create technology. By creating standards and regulatory laws, our lawmakers not only can change how we use a particular technology but also require us to come up with new technology. One example is the environmental regulations in California, demanding a steep reduction in car emissions. Similar acts are enforced in the EU too. When these regulations were made into law, low-emission car engine technology was not available, and the global car industry was forced into creating new technology. A number of innovations were made in a relatively short period of time – from hybrid electric cars to fuel additives.

Similar examples apply to other industries. Anti-pollution regulations have been enforced in most of Europe and North America, providing a large number of innovations[10].

The general consensus in the western world that the death toll from traffic accidents is way too high, has resulted in new policies about speed, safety and driving behaviour. These in turn have led to a number of security-related innovations: streetlights, physically separated driving lanes, airbags, electronic monitoring and alerts, and distance meters to name but a few. Without policies, many of these innovations may not have been around.

In security, we also see how policies spur innovation. Privacy regulations in Europe, and increasingly around the world, create new technology: assessment tools to see how "our system" compares to the regulation, forget-me tools to allow people to be forgotten by the system, information security management systems to monitor and control our implementation of privacy controls, and so on.

Just like Thor's tribe mate who forced a policy change, technology and our use of it forces changes in our policies. The changes in the policies then change the way people use technology, and it also may change the technology itself as we have just seen.

---

[10] Since the introduction of modern anti-pollution regulations, for instance, we've seen an astonishing increase in green technologies, including more efficient solar cells, whole windfarms, more powerful electric and hybrid cars, and so on. Even traditionally non-green technologies like car engines have improved efficiency in order to compete as a 'greener alternative'.

Since culture is defined as the ideas, customs and social behaviours of a particular people or group, we now understand that our surroundings are important factors to consider when we want to work with security culture. Although changing only one part of the triangle will change culture, it makes sense to analyse just *how* that change will impact the other two. It also makes sense to set out to use all three elements: when implementing a new policy, make sure you teach the people in your organisation to understand the change and the reason for it, and use technology to help enforce the change.

In the next chapter I take a closer look at security awareness, and how it relates to security culture.

CHAPTER 3: HOW DOES SECURITY CULTURE RELATE TO SECURITY AWARENESS?

In this chapter, we look at how security culture comprises security awareness, and how security culture succeeds where awareness alone is doomed.

In the previous chapter I discussed how security culture is more than people and competence; culture includes the rules, laws and regulations, as well as the technology we use. Security awareness belongs in the people and competence part of the triangle.

Security awareness is a limited area, as well as a poorly defined one. There is no commonly agreed upon definition of security awareness, which in turn means that a common understanding of what security awareness really is, is non-existent. Almost everyone I talk to has their own idea of what security awareness is, and how to create awareness.

The range of ideas for building security awareness goes from using baseball bats to enforce a certain behaviour on one side, via running boring, generic and non-yielding security awareness trainings, to not doing anything at all. What is even worse is the fact that very few of these efforts are being measured; they are at best measured by anecdotal proof: "I did this, and it did/did not work." Metrics are simply being waved off as "impossible to measure awareness".

For the sake of clarity, I will use the following definition of awareness in this book:

"Knowledge or perception of a situation or fact."
(Oxford dictionary)

What does it mean to have knowledge or perception of a situation or fact? It boils down to two things: the right competence, and the ability to apply said competence in a particular situation.

So far, so good. Building competence can be done; we see that all around us where we learn new skills and information almost daily. The human mind is an amazing machine when it comes to collecting, analysing and using new information and skills. The more we know, the easier it is for our brain to do even more, which is truly amazing[11].

The flipside is that if you learn the wrong skills, outdated information and erroneous mental patterns, your brain still does a great job but just turns out the wrong answers and responses.

---

[11] The psychologists Gigerenzer, Kahneman and Pinker (among others) have developed a variety of models that reflect how humans make decisions, learn new things, and so on. For instance, Kahneman received the Nobel Prize for his work on Prospect Theory, which describes how humans make decisions where the probabilities of certain outcomes are known. Using heuristic processes, humans combine disparate data in order to refine their decisions, even where the individual is unaware or oblivious to the fact that they have this information. (Kahneman and Tversky, "Prospect Theory: An Analysis of Decision Under Risk", 1979.)

3: How Does Security Culture Relate to Security Awareness?

Let us quickly visit the brain and how it works. Take a look around you. Chances are that there is a cup of coffee, tea or other beverage nearby. For the sake of simplicity, I will call it a cup of coffee.

Take a look at the cup. The light that reflects on the object is caught by light-receptors in your eyes. The receptors pick up the wavelengths of the light, and different receptors pick up different wavelengths. The receptors trigger events that are sent down nerve paths into your brain. The light has been transformed into chemical signals.

When the different chemicals reach your brain, your brain recreates an image of the object (that cup of coffee) using one of two methods[12]:

- Slow: You have never seen anything like a cup of coffee before, and your brain does not know what it sees. Your brain slows down and starts to create a mental image, a pattern – what we call a mental pattern – of the object and its significance. Since this is a new observation, your brain may or may not register important properties of the object, such as it has black content, it is hot, it carries liquid, there is only one opening, the handle is there to hold the cup, the liquid is drinkable, the liquid is a drug and so on. To make your brain understand all of these details, it must be taught. You must teach it the significance of the properties, and help it eliminate the non-important ones like the colour of the cup, the size of the table and the form of the room. This slow processing and

---

[12] This example is derived from Kahneman's *Thinking Fast and Slow.*

learning that takes place in your brain requires a large amount of energy (viewed from your brain's perspective), and so it prefers a quicker, faster and less expensive way of processing information.

- Fast: Most of the time, your brain interprets information using a fast method. In this scenario, the object that your brain receives of the coffee cup is matched to an already existing mental pattern in your brain. Your brain recognises the object as a cup and automagically interprets that cup to mean hot, black liquid that helps you (your brain) to be sharper and quicker. This processing takes very little energy (again, from the perspective of your brain), and is lightning fast (compared to the slow function before). No wonder your brain prefers this one!

Now that we have taken a very shallow crash-course in human sensing, perception and information handling, it is time to look at how this functioning also works against us.

Growing up in Europe, I have a thing for ice-cream. During summer holidays, I love to cool down with a cone, or on special occasions a soft ice fresh from the counter. A soft ice in Europe is usually white, tastes of vanilla and you can have it dipped into a variety of powders, colours and liquids. Personally, I prefer a topping of chocolate powder. I observe others who have rainbow sprinkles, some have strawberry sprinkles and others again choose liquid chocolate that turns into a hard shell on their soft ice.

Imagine a hot summer day. The sun is burning, and you are walking through a city centre as a tourist. You see a shop promoting soft ice, and you watch happy, smiling people licking their soft ices as they pass you on the street. "The perfect day for a soft ice," you think, and head to the counter.

Suddenly you discover there are three choices of soft ice. You can have the white soft ice. You can have the brown soft ice. Or you can choose the green soft ice. Let the drooling begin!

Before you choose, keep the image in your mind and tell me: what taste do the different coloured soft ice have? The white one is vanilla, right?

A brown-coloured soft ice-cream. What taste is that? Chocolate? Or sweet beans?

What taste does the green one have? Pistachio nuts (either chemical or real)? Or is it green-tea taste?

Write your answer on a piece of paper. Your answer depends on a lot of things, all learned!

Firstly, your mental image of a soft ice-cream was stored in your brain, and was brought out just by thinking about it. Along with the image, you may also have felt the summer heat, you may have recalled the smells and taste from that memory, and possibly you heard the noises and sounds that you experienced when you had that soft ice. This is your brain going on fast mode. It has learned what soft ice is and the surroundings that go together with it. Every time you think of soft ice, it brings these memories out.

This processing is really good, because you can recall, recognise and act upon a particular situation: summer, vacation, soft ice. Properly trained, this could be you recognising a phishing scam, a Trojan or a threatening situation.

Secondly, your mental image of the soft ice represents what we can call acquired taste. Your answers to the question of colours and the taste each colour must represent are dependent on your culture. If, like me, you are a westerner who grew up and spent most of your time in Europe, Australia or North America, you have learned that when it comes to sweets, and ice-cream in particular, white is likely to mean vanilla, brown to be chocolate and green to be pistachio nut flavour.

Now recall the scenario of me in front of that counter, having the choice of vanilla, chocolate or pistachio. Of those, I would choose chocolate first, pistachio second and vanilla third. So what do I order?

This is where context matters. Am I about to order a soft ice in Europe? Australia? Or in North America? Or am I somewhere else? And if I am somewhere else, do the rules I know, the mental patterns I have learned, still apply?

In fact, I am in Kyoto in Japan. I had a one-day excursion to this fantastic city during my first visit to Japan some years ago. Since I had been in Japan for a few days already, I had picked up on their different idea of sweets. Some I loved, and some I found very hard to understand. So, before I ordered, I asked what kind of flavours they had, and was given the answer: plain (vanilla), sweet beans and green tea.

I probably did look surprised, because I was really expecting the answer to be vanilla, chocolate and pistachio. I expected these particular answers due to one of the characteristics of mental patterns: they get stronger every time we use them. So every time I have seen brown ice cream with the taste of chocolate, that particular mental pattern grew stronger in my mind until the pattern became so strong that anything that no longer fitted into the pattern surely must have been wrong, impossible, or both.

This is sometimes referred to as the Expert Bias[13]. Experts are experts in their particular field because they have had the opportunity to narrow their area of focus, and work mainly in that field so long that their mental patterns are strong and efficient. The flipside they (and those around experts) may experience is the expert's lack of ability to see things from other perspectives – their mental patterns are so strong that they can no longer review their position.

Similar mechanisms apply to people who are not given the opportunity to have their current mental patterns challenged. If you grow up in a particular culture, and you are not exposed to other cultures, it becomes very hard for you to understand that other people may behave differently from you, and that their behaviour may not be malintent or even wrong.

There I was in Kyoto, by this time knowing that brown is sweet beans and not chocolate. My brain, craving for the chocolate flavour, quickly convinced me that sweet bean flavour cannot be that bad and is probably almost as good as chocolate. I ordered a brown soft-ice cone without toppings.

Still expecting chocolate, my brain almost shut down when my taste buds sent the taste from my mouth to my

---

[13] This is also called the 'Curse of Knowledge', and extends beyond expertise and into the difficulties of reasoning with someone else's beliefs. In the words of Birch and Bloom, "adults' own knowledge of an event's outcome can compromise their ability to reason about another person's beliefs about that event." (Susan Birch and Paul Bloom, "The Curse of Knowledge in Reasoning About False Beliefs", 2007.)

brain. I could not believe what I had. I tried several times, and each time the same happened: my brain expected a different taste, and the difference was too great to conceive. All my brain could do was tell me that this did not fit the pattern, this was not right, this was wrong!

I experienced a strong case of cognitive dissonance, a psychological phenomenon that happens when your brain expects something particular to happen, and something else happens instead. It is like your brain just says, "This cannot be. I don't believe this." And then it just denies any of the novelty.

Cognitive dissonance[14] is important in awareness too. If your security awareness programmes are not properly aligned to your organisation's particular needs, they are more likely to create similar responses in your participants that I had in Kyoto. More importantly, I understood the context, and I knew about these effects. Even then, I fell victim to this mental process. We all do, more often than we like to admit.

Part of our job as security officers is to help our colleagues understand risk and teach them appropriate responses. To do that, we need to understand how our human mind functions, so that we can adapt our training efforts to build knowledge and perception to deal with security issues in the correct manner.

---

[14] Cognitive dissonance can be described as the state of having inconsistent thoughts, beliefs or attitudes. In general, it is a mechanism by which a person rationalises conflicting experiences or knowledge, without having to accept that these are, in fact, at odds. (Leon Festinger, *A theory of cognitive dissonance*, 1957.)

3: How Does Security Culture Relate to Security Awareness?

Understanding our brain's shortcuts and mishaps should also help you to understand that it is not your employees who are stupid, it is a question of how we communicate with them that matters.

The main difference between security awareness and security culture is that culture is more than just awareness. If you recall from *Chapter Two*, security culture is a combination of people, policy and technology. Awareness is only about people, and only a subset of the people: it is knowledge only. This does not mean we do not need awareness. Awareness, or competence as I prefer to call it, is vital for people to have to do the right thing. The key is to consider competence as one way of building culture, not an end in itself.

Security awareness in itself only helps people *know about*, or be aware of, the security issue you are training in. Knowing something is not the same as changing a behaviour, which is usually what we want to do when we train people about phishing attempts, password security or clean-desk policies. Knowing about an issue is only *one* of the steps towards changing that behaviour. Using the Social learning theory[15], we discover that there is a four-step cognitive process people use to learn:

1. Attention
2. Retention
3. Reproduction
4. Motivation.

[15] Bandura and Walters, 1963

Each of these steps is important, and awareness is often mostly about the first two.

What does this mean in practice? Let us take a closer look at each of the four elements:

Attention

Attention is about the learner paying attention to the activity to learn. The one who is learning must be present, pay attention and take an interest in what is going on. As in life in general, there are things that impact this step: the learner himself, as well as the training and content.

To enhance attention, we can provide relevance to the learner by explaining why this training behaviour is important. We can also provide an environment where the behaviour we want is already modelled, and show this modelled behaviour.

Security awareness programmes that stop at this level are recognised by measuring attendance only; they report on the number of people taking a particular course.

Retention

Retention is about the learner's ability to retain information. Again, the learner's abilities are at play, and we can help them retain the knowledge by creating an environment that enables easy learning, adapting the content to the level of knowledge of the learner as well as repeating as necessary.

With security culture in mind, we can adapt our programmes and their content to the needs of the learner by analysing the audience before we develop the actual training content. People are different, and may need different approaches to learn best.

Security awareness programmes that stop at this level are recognised by measuring attendance, and repeating the same training programme at some intervals, like a yearly phishing training programme.

Reproduction

Reproduction is about showing that the behaviour is learned. In this stage, the learner will reproduce the learned behaviour and show that they know what to do and how to do it.

Many awareness programmes stop at this level. They use skill tests, questionnaires and other quality-assessment tools during and right after the training programme, showing some level of reproduction. An example is a phishing training programme where you measure how many learners click on a link during the training and not after.

Motivation

The final step, the target to reach for, is to motivate the learner to reproduce the behaviour consistently outside of the learning situation. The learner is taking into account both formal and informal information to decide whether or not to reproduce a behaviour. Both technology and policies play important roles to motivate the learner. If, for example, you want people to discover and report phishing emails, and your reporting system requires them to file a three-page form, their motivation will be lower. They may very well be aware of the problem and know how to handle it, yet the technology to do so is too much of a burden for them to commit to the behaviour.

Security awareness programmes at this level measure behaviour on a number of levels. They may look at attendance of training courses, but will use that number only as an indicator that there is activity. They will implement tests to measure actual competence, or the ability to reproduce. They also implement other metrics to measure the impact of behaviour on their systems using logs and data analysis.

Organisations that implement programmes at this level use a structural approach that helps them focus on improving their security culture. They may still call what they do security awareness trainings, when in practice they are running successful security culture programmes, building and maintaining the kind of security culture they want.

Looking at the definition of culture again – *the ideas, customs and behaviour of a society or group* – it becomes clear that having *knowledge or perception of a situation or a fact* is not enough if we want to change culture. What we need to do is to identify the ideas, the customs and the behaviour that reside in our organisation today, and consider what ideas, customs and behaviours we *want* in our organisation. Bridging that gap is what our efforts should be all about.

By now you may be wondering if I expect you to do all of this by yourself. I don't. Nor should anybody else. Changing culture is a task done by a number of people, and your job is to be part of that force. In the next chapter I will give you some pointers as to whom to ally with.

Building bridges

Building Bridges

John, the CISO of a large, multinational bank, learned that his colleagues in other parts of the organisation viewed his work and team as a nuisance, a distraction to their own work and a hassle that was forced upon them. "They just don't get it," complained John, "I'm here to secure the business so that we can avoid breaches and downtime, and all they give me are complaints and negativity." John is not alone in facing this challenge. The challenge is to demonstrate a clear business value that resonates with the rest of the organisation, even if plans must be changed along the way.

The first step in this direction is to understand the business, and how business in general functions. As part of that understanding, John realised that security secures the business and reduces risk. The purpose of security is not to remove all risk, nor is it a question of getting in the way of business. "I understood that there cannot be security without business," he told me, "but it very well may be business without security!" After this revelation, John toured the different departments and locations, discussing security issues with department managers, country managers and many more. His focus was not

---

on selling security, but to learn about the challenges each department faced, and to learn how he could change the communication within the bank. He set out to build bridges instead of burning them.

John also learned that he could use help to build his security culture message and to spread it throughout the bank. He reached out to the HR department and involved them in his security culture programme. The HR department are a key resource when working with culture in any organisation, and they are also the specialists when it comes to training programmes. Next, he asked the bank's marketing department if they would help craft a message and the needed collateral to empower his security culture campaigns. At first, he was more than a little sceptical to involve creative people who had no understanding of security. Using arguments like "they are trained in communication", and "by working with you, they will learn security", I convinced him to try it on one campaign at first.

By reaching out and building bridges, John set up a core security culture team with members from his own team, from HR and from marketing. He also invited key people from around the bank to be on an advisory board, who were asked to test campaign ideas, comment on materials and give feedback to enhance the overall performance of the security culture programme.

CHAPTER 4: ASKING FOR HELP RAISES YOUR CHANCES OF SUCCESS

In this chapter I will discuss who to involve, and why, when working with security culture – HR, marketing, management and so on.

Humans are impressive when we consider what we can learn to stay on top of our game. History is a clear tell-tale of what may happen when bright minds bring their heads together to evolve their ideas. Consider people such as Edison, Einstein, Marie Curie and Michelangelo. Look at people such as Sun Tzu, Napoleon and Churchill.

It is easy to think of such bright minds as people who did everything by themselves. When looking at their achievements it quickly becomes clear that they were not alone – they had help. They worked with other people. In fact, they knew how to involve the right kind of people, at the right time, to create the impact they needed.

They owe their success to other people.

When analysing security culture programmes that create success, it quickly becomes clear that such programmes are not one-man shows. Successful security culture is built by involving competence from around the organisation to leverage the competence available. Sometimes it also makes sense to look outside the organisation for inspiration, competence and help.

Asking for help may feel like failure. Especially if you are considered the subject matter expert, the one other people come to for answers. Being the expert may mean being used to having all the answers and that being right is expected. What do you do then, when the landscape changes and your experience no longer seems to apply?

You learn to ask for help. Instead of being the know-all, you become the hub who connects the different kinds of knowledge needed in a modern-day security culture programme. You focus on finding the people who have, or can come up with, the right answers. And you bring these people together in a project to build the culture you want to create.

Success today is like success yesterday: a result of the combined efforts of one or several teams. Building a successful team means understanding how to ask for help, and whom to ask it from.

Building security culture requires a lot more than just information security competence. Technology and policies are a part of security culture, just like people and competence. Your security culture team needs to reflect all the areas of security culture, not only those areas you are confident with.

Security culture is a subculture of the organisational culture, your company culture. As such, security culture should be designed and built together with those in the organisation who deal with organisational culture. In most organisations the responsibility of culture lies with HR. HR in turn receives instructions and direction from management through the company employment policies, the company mission and vision, as well as the existing company culture.

HR knows culture. Setting out to create a new security culture in your organisation requires the involvement of HR, and preferably you want them to actively support and work with you. Your goal is to have HR embrace the security culture programme and implement it as a part of the existing company culture programmes.

Many organisations already have HR involved in security. Many employee on-boarding programmes come with "Read and Sign" security policies, mandatory IT security trainings, and distribution of keys and credentials. Organisations also have off-boarding programmes to ensure the handing off of employee keys, credentials and so on.

Security awareness trainings may also be included in HR-controlled trainings. Awareness trainings under HR are often motivated by compliance more than conformity, and often such training efforts are delegated to the security department.

And here is the challenge: unless the security department has dedicated resources who themselves are dedicated to awareness and culture, the training efforts delivered miss the target. Developing and delivering trainings itself is a specialist field, one sometimes referred to as Instructional Design.

The Association of Training and Development (ATD) has great experience in creating trainers and trainings for workforce development, and they provide their members with a special certification in instructional design. You can think of it as the training industry's Certified Information Systems Security Professional (CISSP). There is a reason for that: developing training programmes for adults, programmes that yield the kind of results you want, is a skill and competence that requires training and practice. Just like working with security is a demanding sector that has its own requirements, creating and delivering trainings is a specialist field.

Working closely with HR will provide you with important insights to how culture is currently built and maintained. Piggybacking on the activities with smart messages to enhance security may be a successful strategy. Only by working with HR can you do that.

HR may also run and manage the security culture programme themselves, freeing up precious time and resources from the security team. Keep in mind your goal: to build and maintain security culture. There is nothing in that goal that does not let HR manage the security culture programme itself!

In addition to competence within areas such as training, security and culture, a successful security culture programme must also be communicated in a way that resonates with the audience. Our security messages must be presented using words, images and anecdotes[16] that make sense to those we are trying to teach. Most of the time, they are not subject-matter experts on security – they do other

---

[16] While anecdotes are sneered at by more analytical people, they provide an excellent method of communicating with a broad audience. Steven Denning presents an excellent discussion of anecdotes as part of his argument for storytelling in business leadership ("Telling Tales", Harvard Business Review, 2004).

things like sales, accounting, production, strategy and management. If we are to make them understand, we need to adjust the way we communicate with them.

We must learn how to communicate. Or, we can ask for help from those who know how to communicate.

Many organisations have a marketing or communication department. The names vary depending on sector and industry, but what you are looking for are those people who create information that explains what your organisation does, where the value lies and why others should care. If your organisation does not have a separate department that does this, find the team that does. Or look outside the organisation. Many companies prefer to buy external marketing services.

The kind of help you are looking for from this resource is divided into two parts:

1. Audience analysis
2. Message crafting.

Any great presenter adapts their presentation style, words and content to the audience. They understand that different people have different needs, focus and interests, and make great efforts forming their message to make it stick with that particular audience. To understand their audience, they will ask the organiser who the target audience is, what level of skills they have, as well as other relevant information like sector, industry, language, age, sex and so on[17].

---

[17] Audience analysis differs subtly between disciplines, but in general recommends a few key features be examined: demographics (who the audience

For an inexperienced organiser and speaker, these questions may seem strange and irrelevant, but it helps the speaker to adjust their content and delivery to ensure as many participants as possible take home their message. And that is what is important: hit home with as many as possible.

Analysing your target audience for your security culture programme follows the same principle: the more you understand your audience, the easier it is to ensure they understand your message. Target audience analysis is also something that marketing departments and advertising companies do for a living. To make the most out of the marketing budgets, the market is segmented into user groups with similar traits, who are then documented and analysed according to their demographics. Depending on the products and/or services sold, psychographics may also be applied. When building security culture, you want to consider both demographics and psychographics when analysing your audience.

Segmentation, or the art of dividing your market into subgroups, in your security culture programme can be done by using departments as segments. You may also choose to segment using other borders: countries, companies, teams, locations, language and so on. Each organisation is different, and may need a different approach.

---

is – age, gender, culture, and so on), attitudes (disposition, beliefs, values), knowledge (what does the audience know about the topic) and environment (how is the information being presented, where is the audience when they receive the information, and so on). Depending on your particular circumstances, these will be more or less involved, and will enable you to tailor your communication to the audience.

When you have segmented your organisation, selected which segment to work with and analysed it, it is time to craft your message.

The second area where your marketing department may help in building and maintaining security culture, is crafting the message you want to send. Their expertise and creativity is a great asset in any programme that needs to communicate a clear message. By asking them to join your security culture workgroup, you can bring their skill-sets to your table, helping you create content that makes sense.

Remember that you are the subject-matter expert on security, and they are brought in as experts on communication. This implies that you need to trust their ideas and instincts, even if their ideas may be outside of your comfort zone. You are not the target audience, someone else is.

With all that said, a word of caution. Being creative and communicators, the marketing department does not know much about security, especially in the beginning of your security culture programme. You are the security expert, and as such you must ensure the message conveyed is correct and aligned with the security culture goals. Creativity is great, as long as it moves the programme in the right direction.

Working with creative people may introduce conflicts. The easiest way to involve creative people is by having a clearly defined scope. Narrow it down early on, and help them stay within the defined boundaries of your scope. Your job is not to say "NO!", but rather to ask them nicely, "So how do you see this idea bringing us closer to our goal?"

If you experience a situation where the communication people have one idea and you have a different one, you may consider testing what works. Set up an A/B test with both ideas, using a subset of your target segment as a testing group. You may have to resort to one-on-one testing and interviews, unless your segment is large enough to create a true blind test.

Testing campaigns before you roll them out to a larger part of the organisation can be done using the 12-week campaign of the Security Culture Framework. Use one campaign to test the content, and the following 12-week period to run the content that gave the best results to the larger audience.

I have also had the not so pleasant task of working with someone creative who never accepted my boundaries. In meetings she would be fine with my objections, whereas later I would receive long emails explaining why I was wrong and she was right. She would also disregard my change requests. It became obvious that this could not continue, and she was quickly replaced. Unfortunately, there is no easy way to tell when to replace someone on your team; it is a call that must be made on a case-by-case basis. Ask yourself if the person is really that annoying, or if it is you who is creating the situation.

Knowing when to ask for help is a skill we all can develop. Knowing whom to ask may be a bit tougher. And knowing how to ask can be tricky too!

Table 1

What	Where
Training Culture Recruiting On-boarding Off-boarding Employee data Organisational overview	HR
Communication Design Audience analysis Marketing PR Crafting messages Analysing results A/B testing	Marketing/communication dept
Finance Sponsor/ambassador Visibility Anchoring Policy sign-off Reporting Strategic planning	C-level management

How to ask for help is dependent on what you need and whom you ask. Asking your chief executive officer to support your security culture programme is different from asking your colleague to patch a server.

To enhance your chance to receive the answer you want, it is helpful to understand the other person's perspective and focus. The more you can help them connect their own dots, the easier it will be for them to understand your question, your needs and therefore their interest in helping you. Think of it as audience analysis, where you look at what is important to this person and their role. Ask yourself questions like:

- what are the major challenges this role/person faces?
- how will my idea/challenge/programme be received?
- how can I adapt my idea/challenge/programme to help the role/person?
- how is my idea/challenge/programme fitting in with their major challenge?

Sometimes it also proves valuable to consider how the other person perceives you as a person: we are more likely to help people we like and connect well with.

The next chapter is dedicated to the psychology of how we are influenced by other people. Use that chapter to better understand other tactics you can apply to build the support you require to build and maintain security culture in your organisation.

Building your team

John, the CISO of a large, multinational bank, had a team of cyber security professionals to help him tackle incidents and run their security operations. His team was highly skilled, from networking engineering to intrusion detection system tuning, from security

---

data analytics to incident response. And they all seemed to love their work. Except when the task of security awareness landed on their table. John thought it had turned into a game within his team to avoid any work with security awareness. He understood that his team's lack of interest in awareness could be due to a number of things:

- Awareness is not considered sexy enough (i.e. not technical).
- A team member not having enough knowledge of awareness.
- Awareness work seems to never be successful, turning anyone working with it into a failure.
- A lack of funding to buy the coolest trainings or content available.

Most of these things can be handled easily enough – as soon as they are recognised. Let's take each point by itself:

- Not considered sexy is a common excuse we receive from technical staff. There are several ways to deal with this issue, including hiring a security culture manager, as is increasingly being done in the Nordic countries (Norway, Sweden and Denmark), who will build, implement and manage a security culture programme. Another option is to use technical tools such as the Social Engineering Toolkit, a tool most techies will relate to and like. Communicating the importance and value of security culture work will also help motivate your team to take it on.

- A team not having enough knowledge of awareness is another challenge we see. Of course, if you do not have enough knowledge of a topic, it is hard to realise just how cool it is, right? To tackle this challenge, training your team in security culture is vital. The aforementioned Security Engineering Toolkit is an excellent way to raise knowledge and build interest. Other ways to show how critical and exciting awareness work can be, is to join or design a Social Engineering Capture the Flag (CTF) event with your team. Also, create an environment where it is easy to plan and execute security culture activities.

- The argument about security awareness never being successful is easily combated with good metrics, and an understanding of human behaviours. Use Metrics module to design and build goals and metrics that matters.

- A lack of funding is a challenge in all work – not just security. To get the funding you want, you will have to fight other departments and projects that may be more business aligned and better at communicating direct and indirect value. Again, metrics matter. And when it comes to securing budgets, communicating business value is critical. Do not expect a huge fund from day one. What is more common is that you must demonstrate results and value over time. Again, Metrics module is your friend. Also, a thinking out of the box, low-cost, use-what-we-have mentality will take you a long way when funding is low.

John had very little funding, and could not hire a full-time security culture officer. Instead, he asked his team for two volunteers to spend 40% of their time over the next three months on security awareness. He offered training in the Social Engineering Toolkit, as well as in the Security Culture Framework, and the three would evaluate the progress after the three months. John was hoping that he would motivate the two members who volunteered to take on the security culture work after the initial three-month trial, yet he had not anticipated just what he would get in return.

The new CultureCrew, as they quickly became known, fell in love with the Social Engineering Toolkit and used it immediately. They set up a Capture-the-Flag event of the security team, an event that became so successful people from outside of security wanted to join and asked when the next event would take place. When the review meeting with John and CultureCrew took place at the end of the three-month evaluation period, John was surprised to hear that both team members would like to go on; they even presented an 18-month plan on how to build security culture company-wide. They explained that the Security Culture Framework offered templates they had used to develop campaigns they could implement easily and with little extra effort, and they had all the resources they needed to start.

After a review and some minor adjustments, John signed off CultureCrew's plan to get their security culture going, knowing that the heart of security operations, his team, had changed their mind completely about security awareness work.

CHAPTER 5: THE PSYCHOLOGY OF GROUPS, AND HOW TO USE IT TO YOUR BENEFIT

In this chapter, we take a look at one of the important psychological mechanisms of humans: groups and social interaction. Learn how to use in-groups to build trust.

A key to success with building and maintaining good (security) culture is to understand that people are different, and that you need to adapt your efforts to *their* needs, backgrounds and knowledge. Successful security culture is built by security professionals who know their own strengths and include relevant personnel and competence from across their organisation.

One of the challenges of our human mind is how we are hardwired to relate and interact with other individuals[18]. We are, as species, a social creature, designed to live in groups. Research in psychology strongly suggests that our grouping behaviour is *built in* in our basic functions. We, humans, cannot survive alone; we rely on our group to feed us, to teach us and to support us. You can observe this need easily in babies and small children: they would

---

[18] Group formation has long been studied in psychology and researchers generally recognise two in-built pressures that provide the impulse to form groups: social cohesion (interpersonal attraction drawing people together) and social identity (mutual identification of some social class, such as culture, employment, hobbies, and so on).

not survive without parents or other grown-ups to feed and care for them.

What is interesting from a perspective of building and maintaining security culture is that as we grow up, we rely as much, perhaps even *more*, on groups. These groups come in different shapes and sizes, and form inter-group relationships. All human beings belong to a number of groups, from your family, extended family, to the school you attended, to the sports team you support, to the workplace and so on. The groups we belong to, are a member of, are referred to as *in-groups* in psychology.[19]

There are an even larger number of groups that we do *not* belong to. Examples can be different families than your own, people in a different workplace, supporters of sports teams you do not support, political groups, as well as cities and countries around the world. Groups we do not belong to are referred to as *out-groups* in psychology[20].

Based on in- and out-groups, we can look at how we interact inside our groups, and how we treat people not from our own groups[21].

Think about your workplace. There are a number of people working there. The organisation where you work is an in-group for everyone who works there. All your

---

[19] Tajfel, Billig, Bundy and Flament, "Social categorization and intergroup behaviour", 1971.

[20] Ibid.

[21] The infamous Stanford Prison Experiment clearly demonstrates how groups can be formed rapidly and coerced into applying significant pressure against out-groups.

colleagues, across the organisation, share the same in-group. The larger your organisation, the more complex it becomes, and the more likely it is that smaller groups of people form: workgroups, teams, departments, locations and so on. Each member of these *subgroups* share the common in-group of the organisation, and they create new in-groups based on the new subgroup.

To use an example: you and your team, and everyone else in your organisation, form one in-group: the employer. You and your team are also members of a subgroup of that group: your department. Everyone inside your department shares this in-group with you, and no-one else in your organisation does. Your department becomes an in-group, and every other department becomes an out-group. And for all the other departments in your organisation, your department is an out-group: you are not with them, you are an outsider, possibly even an enemy.

You can continue to create subgroups inside the department, and you will see that every team, project and group of people form and take part in a number of different in-groups. And, consequently, are considered a member of numerous out-groups.

Forming groups is a very good strategy to create greater results than can be achieved alone, a strategy seen in many other creatures. To make groups effective, each individual is required to give up some of its own power and resources to the mutual benefit of the group. We pay a membership due by accepting to obey certain rules, to follow the commands and so on. In return we are supported by the others, as well as being defended from outside threat. This is sometimes referred to as a *social contract*[22].

This outside threat is important. Any out-group is considered a potential threat, no matter how weak we consider the group to be. Also, no matter how weak our affiliation is with our in-group, our mind is biased when meeting and dealing with people who are not members of our in-group. It's almost like we automatically jump into the trenches and start firing at anything they say or do.

Understanding how strong our social bonding is when it comes to our ability to connect with others, will help us to change our behaviours when we meet with and try to engage people in our out-groups. It also helps us understand why some groups of people are difficult to connect and bond with. As the security professional, it is part of your job to interact with all the different groups in your organisation. Realising that some of the difficulties you encounter with other people may be due to how the human mind is wired, and not about you personally, may help you do a better job.

With the backdrop of in-groups and out-groups, you are now ready to figure out how to handle the challenges created by these social bonds. Knowing that each department forms an in-group, effectively enforcing a hostility towards anyone not in that department, will help

---

[22] Social contract theory extends across a number of disciplines, including psychology, philosophy, political science and sociology, and describes an implicit agreement within a group that determines the rights and responsibilities of the group and its members. Notable writers on the topic include Thomas Hobbes, John Locke and Jean-Jacques Rousseau.

you come up with a strategy of using social contracts and group membership to build security culture.

Knowing about in-groups, and the biases we have, points towards a solution: make yourself and them members of the same group, turning on the in-group bias for all of you. The good news is that you already share one such in-group: your employer, the organisation you all work for. So, the first step towards building security culture is to create a strong company culture: a common ground for all the employees, an "us" mentality. Successful enterprises have used this knowledge for decades. Think of brands like Coca-Cola, IBM and Google. They all share one important thing: they have formed and cultivated a company-wide identity, forming an in-group of all the employees.

On the start-up scene you see the same strategy applied: by building a strong brand awareness, first internally, later externally, the employees feel a strong connection to the business. This connection creates a sense of purpose that enables the company to build a strong internal culture, an in-group that is used to tackle any challenge and struggle that comes their way.

Organisational culture is very often the responsibility of HR. Just like any other department, HR itself forms a subgroup, an in-group sharing all the properties of groups. You, the security professional, are most likely not part of their in-group. As you just learned, that means you are more likely to be met with suspicion and hostility when approaching them. Remember that this is not a deliberate attitude, it is a bias all human beings succumb to.

5: The Psychology of Groups, and How to Use it to Your Benefit

> In organisations without a strong corporate identity, there is a likelihood of compartmentalisation: departments, and possibly teams, have formed their own strong in-group cultures, trumping that of the organisation. In such organisations, all the in-group biases are being enforced, creating a culture of suspicion, hostility and change-resistance[23].

Working with HR is key to successfully building and maintaining security culture. Your ultimate goal should be to incorporate security culture as a part of the organisational culture: you want security culture to be a natural part of the culture in your organisation.

If you do not already have a good relationship with HR, this is the time to start. Using what you just read about groups, start bonding with HR. There are two main strategies to apply:

1. Create a strong company culture, where everybody pulls in the same direction.

2. Build a new subgroup, where you include people from the relevant groups you want to interact with.

Most of the time, you will find it easier to start with building a new subgroup, and leverage that to build organisation-wide change.

There are many tactics you can use to create new subgroups: you can appear at the coffee machine used by the group you want to influence, forming a new informal

---

[23] Neville Symington identifies this form of conflict as a type of narcissism, describing "organizations so riven by narcissistic currents that [...] little creative work was done". (Symington, *Narcissism: A New Theory*, 1993.)

group; you can establish a new project involving people from the department(s) you want to influence, forming a formal group; you can combine these tactics in mixed-level interactions.

The Security Culture Framework impacts culture on several levels through the way it leverages in-group biases. Think of the core team as a cross-department group that forms a new in-group with a group mission to change the culture of the organisation. As the work progresses, this cross-department project builds new subgroups that create change in how things are done, effectively impacting the organisational culture. Each training that is completed by employees form new subgroups comprising the new competence and expected behaviour your core team set out to create.

Over time, with repeated messages across a number of channels, a new culture is forming, replacing the existing culture[24].

Trying to change culture without understanding the force of group bias is very tough. You can use the power of groups to build support across departments, and to learn about particular challenges other groups face in their day-to-day jobs.

Fortunately, we are not supposed to do everything ourselves. We are social creatures, which enables us to

---

[24] In sociology, this constant shifting of cultures and the movement of ideas and traits between cultures inevitably results in the development of new, distinct cultures. It does not describe the origin of a culture, in the sense that no culture springs up fully-formed – all cultures are adaptations of earlier cultures, and all cultures will inevitably change and become something else. (Wendy Griswold, *Cultures and Societies in a Changing World,* 1994.)

reach out to others for help. The power of groups is profound.

As the Organisation module of the Security Culture Framework states, your core workgroup should include resources from HR and marketing in addition to security. Already, you have a new group that bridges the gap between three different departments. This group also makes it easier for you to succeed in your job, as it will likely introduce you to other security challenges these departments face.

If your resources allow for it, you can also include other people in your core group. Another way to use the group bias to build your success is to set up specific taskforces.

Imagine a department that is especially challenging with how they treat you and security. They have formed a strong, negative opinion towards the services you provide, and do their best to figure out how to avoid your involvement in their systems and policies.

You have tried to reason with them, and you have tried to apply the organisational-wide policies. This department is not paying attention, and instead they are doing what they can to sabotage your security efforts. You are quickly running out of options.

This is a common situation. Often our gut response is aggression – and so is theirs. Aggression creates stale boundaries, where the trenches form and dialogue stops. Instead of working towards a common good, we find each other fighting.

It is hard to change this response, which is a manifestation of group bias, yet it is our responsibility to solve these fights for the good of the organisation. Again, the best strategy to apply relies on forming new in-groups. Groups you can use to establish communication, through which you can form an understanding of their side of the story. Groups you should use to build trust.

You may have to take it slow, and accept their rejection: if the conflict has evolved into the trenches, building trust and communication may be time consuming[25]. Your first steps should be to establish a common ground, where you invite the other party to discuss their perspective. Do not object, and avoid judgement. Let them talk. Make them talk. Make them commit to one thing only: agree to meet again!

What you just did was to form a new group. A group you are a member of. A group where both parties participate and where you are all together. Use this group to form a strong group identity, an identity you can leverage later in the process.

Understanding group bias, and how we all succumb to it, will make you better at building and maintaining security culture. Your ultimate goal is to build a company-wide security culture. As you have seen in this chapter, some of that work must be done through the active use of groups and projects. Build trust and relationships on all levels throughout your organisation. Ask for help, ideas and feedback. Most people will gladly talk to you and share

---

[25] There are a number of valid approaches and strategies for dealing with conflicts; for a more nuanced and detailed overview, conflict management theory offers a wide range of options applicable to almost any field or industry. *The International Journal of Conflict Management* provides a wealth of information and analysis of conflict management, and is published quarterly.

insights. And those bonds you make walking and talking are new groups: in-groups that give you the power to create better culture and easier change.

People who like you, consider you as part of one or more of their in-groups. The group bias tells us that members of our groups are more likely to help us. Reach out to them!

In the next chapter, you will learn about measuring culture and how you can see behaviour in your own systems.

The story of non-functioning awareness

John, the CISO of a large, multinational bank in Europe, had a mounting feeling that he had forgotten something. He looked through his pockets, found his keys, his smartphone, a few coins and his access card. Everything was present. He sat in his office to read the threat reports he received from the computer emergency response team every morning, and everything seemed fine. John asked his colleague Peter for an update on the progress of the pushout of the latest patch for the online banking security system.

The phone rang as Peter entered John's office to update his boss. There was a blink of panic in John's eyes as he suddenly remembered what he had forgotten: a sales meeting with the awareness training provider they had used the past two years. He picked up the phone, listened and said, "Yes, thanks, I will be right down."

Peter smiled, shook his head and said, "John, you really should take some time off! You could use it!"

John smiled back and replied, "Right, you know what this job is like. When was the last time you took some time off?" before he rushed out of his office.

A few minutes later, he had installed himself and Sheila, the salesperson he loved for her easy answers and great service, in one of the meeting rooms with windows overlooking the city far below. Sheila asked if he had had the time to consider what kind of awareness focus the bank needed this year, and was not surprised when he admitted that he had not looked into that yet. She pulled out a glossy brochure, and told him all about their latest offering. John did not notice anything new since last year, except a possible change in the colours. Or perhaps it was the same ones. He could not tell.

Later that day, John was back at his desk wondering if he had made the right choice when he just reordered the same training programme from Sheila that he had used the past three years. According to Sheila, there were some additions to the training programme to reflect the recent password breaches and the new spear phishing attacks. When asked how he could measure the success of the programme, his training vendor offered a number of metrics:

- Total number of trainings distributed.
- Total number of trainings opened.
- Total number of successfully completed trainings (here, John wondered if this was just a record of everyone who had clicked through the slides).

John had the metrics from earlier years, and Sheila said they looked ok. What nagged John was that even with trainings every year, the number of breaches were on the rise. His security metrics showed a trend towards more people clicking on phishing links, and an increasing number of malware being detected in the bank's systems. Were the metrics the training company provided simply wrong? Did they show something else? What do the present metrics really tell me, John pondered. After some reflection, John realised he needed help.

The challenge John had is one we see with many security awareness programs – vanity metrics, a coin termed by Eric Ries in his book *The Lean Startup*. Vanity metrics are numbers, reports and statistics that seemingly provide value, but on closer inspection don't give us any information that we can use to analyse our scope. Vanity metrics are just nice numbers, with little or no meaning. In other words, the numbers John got from his training supplier gave no meaning by themselves; they did not give him any information about the change in behaviour that the trainings were supposed to give. To solve this challenge, John had to come up with metrics that would give him real information that was relevant and on target.

We devised a plan where John first had to define a set of target behaviours he wanted in the employees. Next, we had to translate those behaviours into something he could measure on his computer systems and networks. Finally, he had to set up a baseline metric, using the measures defined, so he could compare the results of his security awareness program.

By following this plan, John decided that he wanted to focus on one behaviour only, a wise choice if resources are limited or you are setting out to do something new. The behaviour he chose was phishing detection and avoidance. Later, he also added what he called "Safe Rescue" to his behaviours, a mechanism in employees that if they had been breached, they would promptly turn to the information and communications technology support with their computer, to have it assessed and cleaned. He named this particular behaviour Safe Rescue because he realised how important it was for employees to feel safe and secure in the handling of a successful phishing attack.

Now that John knew what behaviour he wanted to change, he could look at how to measure that particular behaviour. Using his team and their technical knowledge, they identified existing systems and logs they could use to collect the number of incoming phishing attempts. A challenge they faced was how to measure successful phishing attacks. They decided to use the number of compromised systems, and that 10% of compromised computers were due to successful phishing. That definition allowed them to measure the change in compromised systems, and use the fluctuation as an indicator of successful phishing.

John and his team came to the understanding that most compromised systems were not reported by the user, and made the hypothesis that people were afraid of reporting a successful phishing attack – people were not willing to accept and report that they had clicked on a malicious link, or opened a bad attachment. This is when John added Safe Rescue to his behaviour target. He realised that he needed two things: a metric of actually compromised systems from phishing, and users who were not afraid of reporting a compromised system. The former would help him better understand his metrics and provide better reports to management. The latter would create a culture where compromised computers were quickly reported and managed, effectively increasing the overall security of the bank. He also realised that users who approached support with their compromised systems would create a metric that he could use to learn of trends in phishing as well as measure users' behaviour.

With the target behaviours defined, John could use the metrics he had devised to create a baseline. And that is what he did.

CHAPTER 6: MEASURING CULTURE

In this chapter I will look at a few ways to measure culture, and how you can take existing data to use as a baseline.

One thing I often hear from fellow security professionals is that it is impossible to measure awareness and culture. It is an interesting point of view, and one that is usually based upon:

- not knowing how to measure soft skills.

- previous failures to create results from awareness activities.

It often boils down to not realising that awareness and culture are reflected in the behaviours of employees. In most organisations today, the heavy use of computer systems enables us to closely monitor any and all use. An example:

> Bob, a salesperson who has been in your organisation for two years in March, uses a combination of a laptop, a pad and his smartphone to interact with the computer systems. He reads his emails, he uses customer relationship management software, he registers his expenses and so on. All of these systems are set up to log every interaction with users, John's included. The purpose of the logging is to ensure high-quality service, backtrack activities to see if

there was something a particular user did to cause problems, and receive early warnings on potentially disastrous changes in the computer systems.

Every time Bob uses the systems, his data is being recorded: timestamped, geolocated, device used, system used and so on. These logs show Bob's current behaviours, including his habit of eating his lunch at a café down the road. Of course, you do not know that he is eating his lunch there, what you know is that his device, using his credentials, is being used almost daily to connect from that location.

What you see is *how* Bob is using the computer systems. That is what social scientists call behaviour. Bob is interacting with his surroundings, and you are logging that interaction. You are measuring his behaviour.

Bob's employer has a bring your own device (BYOD) policy, stating that connection to the computer systems must only occur using a virtual private network, and the use of public Wi-Fi is not allowed. When on the road, Bob should only rely on his mobile Internet connection.

When you examine the connection logs for the sales team, you discover that most of John's colleagues fail to follow the policy. Instead of using their mobile network, they prefer to connect from Wi-Fi networks on the road.

Using the current log data, you now have a baseline behaviour. You know your current situation, the "as is".

The baseline measurement is important when designing change: knowing where you are makes it possible to navigate to the location you need to be. If you know where you want to be, that is.

In John's organisation, the goal state is described in the policy document:

Every worker outside our premises should connect using VPN, and only through mobile networks or previously accepted networks.

In this case, defining your goal is quite easy: you need employees to connect to the computer systems with VPN, and from pre-defined networks only. You also know that Bob and his colleagues are far from this goal; their behaviour is not according to your goal.

The baseline measurement shows a clear gap from your defined goal. That gap is what you will bridge with your security culture programme. Using the Security Culture Framework, you are now ready to take a closer look at Bob and his colleagues, analysing their behaviour, their current security understanding and their preferred communication style. Next, you choose activities that will resonate with Bob, helping him understand *why* he needs to follow the company policy.

Part of your analysis should be to interview Bob, possibly even going out on the road with him for a day, so you can better understand the situation from his perspective. He might tell you that the mobile network is so slow that it makes it impossible to do his job. Maybe he is unaware of his phone automatically connecting to open Wi-Fi networks, There are a number of possible explanations for Bob's current behaviour, and understanding his side will provide you with a better idea of how to change it.

After creating your baseline and analysing Bob's current behaviour, you create a security culture campaign, using the Security Culture Framework, with a selection of different activities, all directly related to Bob and his team's needs. Your programme consists of a six-week nano-learning programme with two five-minute video clips each week. You also join two sales meetings, one at the start of the programme and one towards the end, where you use a Pineapple device to demonstrate what a man-in-the-middle attack may look like, surprising everyone attending at just how easy it is to intercept traffic. You also distribute a keyring with the text "Lock My Door". Before you start the programme, you run a short five-question survey where employees are asked about their general security knowledge. You rerun the same survey a week after your programme finishes, giving you another source of information that you can correlate with your logs.

After your security culture campaign has come to an end, you take another look at your logs where you discover a steady change in how the sales department connect to the main systems. Most of the sales force now connect using VPN and the mobile networks while on the road.

> You also notice that Bob no longer seems to have his lunch at that diner. Looking at the geolocation data your logs collect, you notice he is connecting from one of the subsidiaries, where he gets access to a high-speed Internet connection without breaking the company policy.
>
> Comparing the results from your two runs of the survey, you also notice a clear change in the security knowledge and understanding of the sales team. They show a clear trend towards understanding why the policies are in place, and that even though the policies demand a behaviour that to the salespeople seems counterproductive (getting in the way of their work), they now realise that if they fail to follow the policies, they effectively put the workplace in danger.

The argument that it is very hard to measure awareness and behaviour change is flawed[26]. Just like anything else, it comes down to your current knowledge and skill-set. If you have never learned how to look for behaviour data in your systems, you are not to blame. I hope that reading this chapter has spawned a few ideas as to how you can use your own data sources to look for behavioural data.

Using your current data sources is a great way to look at how behaviour translates into patterns in your logs. There is usually no need to buy another system or software to

---

[26] There are a number of methods, techniques and principles on measuring behaviour and change available to social scientists. The UK's Government Social Research office published a report describing models for measuring behavior change in a report entitled "Reference Report: An overview of behaviour change models and their uses" (2008).

create more data when you want to measure awareness and behaviour change. Most organisations I work with have more than enough data points and logs are readily available. Sometimes you need to turn on a logging feature in the system. Most of the time, however, the challenge is to select just the right data to use from the abundance of available data.

Another challenge that sometimes arises is the need to do proper analysis on the data. Not every security professional is also a skilled data analyst. Most security professionals are not social scientists. We, the security professionals, tend to come from a hard-science background, where only what we see directly is considered an acceptable truth.

When it comes to understanding people, behaviour, awareness and culture, we need to learn from the social scientists. There are a number of scientific tools and methods used by psychologists, sociologists and anthropologists around the world. These include both quantitative data (think of your logs) and qualitative data (think of an awareness survey or maturity model). Arguments still rage about which one of these methods is best when understanding people: the current consensus is that we need both methods to create a more complete understanding of how we behave and how change can be controlled.

The understanding that we may need both quantitative and qualitative data to create a wider understanding of behaviour and change is important to notice in security culture. Your logs tell so much (or so little), and surveys are biased by both the questions and their wording, as much as by the context and understanding of the participants. Understanding that both quantitative data and qualitative data can lead you far away from your path will help you look for ways to assure the quality of the data, and its validity to the real world, as quickly and early as possible. Correlating quantitative data with qualitative data may help you discover discrepancies and problems with your hypothesis.

Where do you look for data?

You can use a number of different sources for information on behaviour – either directly or indirectly. Your budgets may impose limits (as they should), and so may your own interest and skill-set. A data analyst is a great asset to any security team, and can identify relevant data sources as well as creating the necessary analysis.

In the book *Data-Driven Security*, Jay Jacobs and Bob Rudis walk the reader through how to set up and run your own security analytics using R and Python. In their dashboard chapter, they include an example of a CISO dashboard on security awareness based on the SANS awareness maturity survey. I strongly suggest reading that book, even if you are not a data analyst. Their clear explanations based on real security issues make it very easy to relate to the topic, making it fun to learn!

Most computer systems today come with immense logging opportunities, giving you vast amounts of data to analyse your employees' behaviours on your systems. Often, all it takes is knowing where to look, and turning the logging on.

Surveys can provide a lot of information. There are also a number of challenges with surveys, including the fact that it takes some communication skills to create quality surveys[27] that yield the results you need, and not only what you want. My opinion is that smaller surveys are better than larger ones when it comes to security awareness. Most people in your organisation are not as passionate about security as you are, so making them answer a long survey is usually harder than having them answer three or four questions.

An alternative to surveys are interviews. Interviews require more resources (they take time and are one-on-one) than surveys. The upside with interviews is that you can pick up other information from the participant, and you may discover information otherwise kept from you.

Interviews can be conducted in a number of different ways, depending on your purpose. You can do the coffee-machine interview with a great number of people, where you will ask a couple of questions in an informal way to random people you meet. This may help you discover issues you are not currently aware of, and may be conducted over some time. These kinds of interviews are cheap (you conduct them when you fetch your coffee), and are best applied to collecting informal data (i.e. what you learn may not be very useful for in-depth analysis) that you can use for careful correlation with other data sources.

---

[27] Surveys are a common method of conducting research, but need to be carefully composed if they are to provide meaningful results. Ideally, a statistician will be available to ensure that results can be appropriately derived from the responses, but this is largely useless unless the correct questions are being asked. Most introductory texts on research methods should have good advice on composing effective surveys.

You may also do formal types of interviews, where you will have a defined set of questions, and where you select the participants based on what you are setting out to learn. You may interview department managers to discover discrepancies in culture between departments, or you may interview all members of a team to learn the team's combined understanding of security.

In addition to internal data sources, you may look for information outside your organisation. Some countries and industries collect security information and create trend analysis reports that may be used to discover how your organisation compares to the industry. You may also use breach report data available for download, and compare it with your own systems and breaches.

Take the opportunity to jump into your own logs and systems. Let the question "How can I see behaviour of my users in this particular log?" guide you through your quest. You may end up becoming another great data analyst, or you may decide that you need someone else to do this job. No matter what you decide, I guarantee you that you will find ways to track behaviour. Then ask yourself the next question: "What other logs can I combine this with, and what will I then learn?"

A word of warning: you may find yourself digging deeper and deeper, and forgetting about why you are looking for a particular dataset. There is so much to be discovered in the logs!

In the next chapter I introduce the Security Culture Framework, and present one way to set up a security culture programme that yields results.

CHAPTER 7: BUILDING SECURITY CULTURE

In this chapter we take a look at the Security Culture Framework, and explain how a methodology helps organisations develop and maintain good security culture.

Building and maintaining security culture is like any other process you manage: continuous, planned, controlled and audited. I am sure you are familiar with the PDCA (Plan, Do, Check, Act) flow of process management from the ISO/IEC and other standards. What you may not know is that the same pattern of planning, doing, checking the results and implementing necessary changes (act) also works great when it comes to working with people.

After many years of listening to frustrated security professionals who felt they had failed in building security awareness, I analysed what went wrong. I also wanted to see what successfully implemented programmes had in common. In my travels around the world, I spoke with a large number of security people in a wide variety of organisations of all sizes. Two things quickly became apparent:

1. There are more successful programmes than we realise.
2. The failures could be easily mended by changing the approach.

The first finding is important because it gives us hope, and proof, that building and maintaining security culture is possible, and may not require that much from us.

The second finding is important because it points us in the right direction: by changing the way we design and implement security awareness programmes, we too can be successful.

Next, I looked at what was being done. Again, I found fundamental differences:

- Successful programmes were designed and implemented in the organisation using resources from HR, marketing and communication in addition to the security officer (SO). They leveraged the different competences in the different fields of speciality to set up programmes that actually worked. They also had long-term perspectives, with clearly defined goals, milestones and metrics. And finally, they ran their programmes as projects within a process – following the PDCA cycle.

- Failed programmes came in two broad categories: those where the SO did everything himself, and those who only focus on checkbox compliance.

These findings made it easy to pinpoint the mistakes to avoid, and the best practices to share, and I could create the first iteration of the Security Culture Framework together with Lars Haug and Mo Amin.

The Security Culture Framework is free and open. You can find it at *securitycultureframework.com*, and as with all free and open approaches, it gets better the more people join the discussion, sharing experiences and working on evolving the framework itself.

The Security Culture Framework consists of four parts, making a fully repeatable process. It targets large organisations, and its open and flexible structure makes it easy to adjust to any organisation and size. It is designed to help you organise your work with building and maintaining security culture, and will not replace any of your existing tools, suppliers or materials; you will still need those.

The framework was created to help set up and run your security culture programme – it is not a programme in itself.

The framework consists of four parts:

1. Metrics
2. Organisation
3. Topics
4. Planner.

Each of the parts are tied to the other, and they operate together to form a template of a security culture programme. Depending on where your organisation is today, the starting point is usually one of two: the Metrics, where you would define goals, or the Organisation, where you would set up your team. For the sake of simplicity, I run through each of the parts, and then walk you through one iteration of the programme, starting by setting up a team.

A security culture programme is the combined activities you do to build and maintain security culture in your organisation.

Metrics

The Metrics part of the framework helps you understand what you are setting out to do with your security culture programme.

In this part of the programme you will define your goals – long-term and short-term. You may have different kinds of goals – from specific results goals like "By the end of this year, we will have reduced the number of successful phishing attacks by 50%", to learning goals like "By the end of this programme, the participant will demonstrate how to discover and avoid a phishing attempt."

A question that I get from time to time is "Why do I need to set goals?" The quick answer is that a goal helps you understand where you are supposed to go.

Considering the two kinds of goals just mentioned, both focus on phishing, which helps you determine what kind of activities you should implement in your programme. The result goal is telling you what you want to achieve in the metrics on your systems and reports: a 50% reduction of successful phishing attempts. A result goal used correctly will help you understand where you will find supporting data to document your progress towards your goal.

In this example, there may be a number of different sources in your current system that may provide the metrics you need.

Another pointer that a result goal gives you is to understand your current situation. To reduce the number of successful phishing attempts by 50%, you need to know how many attempts are currently being successful.

You use the goal to help you understand where to find metrics that you can use both to understand your current status and the status of your future.

You may use this basic template to define result goals:

By .... (time/date)

we will have .... (reduced/eliminated/increased/created)

the .... (task/area/topic) by .... (#/%/days).

In the ISO/IEC 27000 series, the current state is defined as "as is", and the future state is defined as "to be". Since you are setting out to change the current state of your organisation, you need a clear understanding of both states. The Metrics module is your reminder to do just that.

The other kind of goal, the learning goal, is designed to help you consider what you want, or sometimes need, your participants to learn. The learning goal should be created to support your result goal, and is defined by asking yourself what participants need to know, do or understand to move from their current state into the state of your goal.

You can use the following basic template to define learning goals:

By the end of this.....................................
(training/course/programme)

the participant will ....
(demonstrate/know/show/understand)

....
(topic/area of knowledge/skill).

Using SMART goals

When defining results goals for your security culture programme, I advise creating so-called SMART goals:

- Specific
- Measurable
- Achievable
- Realistic
- Timed.

SMART goals use a model that helps you create goals that are more likely to succeed. The model forces you to be as specific as you can, adding necessary detail and focus to your goal. By being measurable, a SMART goal helps you know when you have reached the goal. Achievable is a test to see if it is possible to do what you set out to do with the current resources available. Realistic is a quality control to remind you that we set out to do something for real; this is not a dream or a vision. Finally, a SMART goal should have a clearly defined deadline, so that you have something to help you plan towards, as well as a period in time where you can say "We did it!"

One of the challenges many security officers share is the need for more funding for their awareness programmes. Having clearly defined goals, backed by numbers that relate to the business, is a great help to communicate such needs. The Metrics part of the Security Culture Framework helps you better understand how to measure your progress, as well as document your results and needs. It also helps you pinpoint your area of focus, which in turn makes it easier to implement the right kind of activities in your programme.

The Organisation part

As just mentioned, one of the challenges faced by failed awareness programmes was the idea that "I have to do it all by myself." This was in contrast to the successful programmes, which generally involved a larger team with a broad understanding of culture, training, communication and security.

The Organisation part of the Security Culture Framework helps you understand what kind of resources you need in the core security culture workgroup, as well as who else should be involved.

At a minimum, your core workgroup should have the following competencies on board:

- Security
- Communication
- Culture and training.

This often translates to someone from the security office, someone from marketing/communication and someone from HR. With the core competencies in place, you can start planning your programme.

In larger organisations you may want a steering committee who sponsor and govern the programme, and act as the liaison between the programme and top-level management. In smaller organisations, you may report directly to the CEO, chief information officer (CIO) or CISO.

Depending on your chosen goals, you may also include other people in the workgroup. Competencies that often come in handy include:

- training design/instructional design
- graphic design
- copywriting/editing
- data analytics.

Some organisations have these resources internally, and others choose to buy external services.

One point to make is that the core workgroup requires security competence, but that does not mean that the SO must also be the group manager. One very efficient way to handle the workgroup is to use a project manager, or at the very least a project administrator to take the administration, meeting planning and so on off the shoulders of the SO. Remember that the SO's primary role in the workgroup is to provide security competence and guidance, which is not the same as managing the group itself!

Another important aspect of the Organisation is the audience analysis section. People are different, with different interest and areas of focus. Departments are different – they come with different tasks, some of which attract people with special competence and different personality types. Organisations with different locations, including multinationals, may experience that each location has its own particular subculture.

When you design, plan and implement your security culture programme you must understand the differences and similarities of these groups, so you can adapt your activities, goals and expectations to each of the target audiences.

A target audience is the name that we borrow from marketing professionals, set to the group of people we aim our security culture activities at. Unlike what some awareness training companies may tell you, there is no such thing as "One Size Fits All" when it comes to training and communication. To reach your defined goals, you also need to understand what your audience is like, so you can adapt to their needs.

Using the phishing example from before: instead of running a generic phishing training campaign towards all the employees in your organisation, you may analyse who are the most likely targets and who are the most vulnerable targets, and come up with a list of top-level managers, key business developers, key engineers and a few others whom you consider the likelier targets for spear phishing attacks. Based on your list, you create two subgroups: Business Focus and Engineering Focus. Now you have two separate groups, with different characteristics.

The Business group consists of the top-level (and possibly key mid-level) managers plus the business developers, whereas the Engineering group consists of a selection of patent lawyers, key engineers and developers, plus perhaps their assistants.

At this point, it should become clear that although both groups are considered targets for spear phishing attacks and need training, the groups also differ in their interests, area of focus, knowledge and understanding.

Your conclusion should be to create two different campaigns, both with the same overall goal of reducing the total number of successful phishing attacks by 50%, and the *content* and the *activities* of the two campaigns should be different to best communicate with the people in the groups.

For the Business group, you may focus your example phishing attempts on relevant (and current) projects and business development focus. You may write the collateral in words that resonate with their area of focus. For the Engineering group, you will do the same, focusing on examples and words they can relate directly to.

You will reach your goals faster and easier if you help your target audience to quick and painless learning. The more you know about your target audience, the easier it will be for you to adapt the message and content to their particular needs.

Knowing the area of focus and interest of all different target audiences may not be feasible. One strategy I see implemented with great success is to involve the target department or audience in the security culture workgroup for the particular goal. In the preceding example, you could invite someone from the Business target group to advise on what may or may not work in that group, and you could invite someone from the Engineering group to do the same for that target audience. By inviting your target audience into the planning of activities, you are also likely to learn about issues you did not know about, as well as building relations and bridges to people around your organisation who may become your sponsors and advocates.

Topics

So far, using the Security Culture Framework, we have defined one or several clear goals, we understand how to measure them, we have set up a workgroup to organise the programme and we know that we need to adapt our activities to the people we are training.

The next part of the Security Culture Framework is Topics. Building on your defined goal and your understanding of the target audience, the Topics are there to help you choose the kind of activities that ensure a successful security culture programme.

There are no limits to the kind of activities that can be used in building and maintaining culture, and this is where the marketing department may excel in creating content.

Marketing departments are usually well versed in communicating a message in a way that the target audience can relate to in a positive way. Let them go crazy with their creativity. Just a fair bit of warning: marketing people usually know how to build great communication campaigns, but they may not understand security. You need to be in control of the overall message, and remind your creative allies what the goal is. One tip is to ask the following question: "How exactly is this activity taking us closer to the goal?" If you are happy with their answer, go with it. If not, you may want to follow up with "What can we change to align it to our goal?"

To help you get going with what can be used as activities, consider this list as a starting point:

- e-learning
- Nano-learning
- Classroom training
- Lunch & learn
- Breakfast sessions
- Demonstrations (live and recorded)
- Knowledge Pills
- Google Hangouts
- Question and answer sessions
- FAQ
- Gamification (done properly!)
- Posters
- Stickers
- Giveaways.

One of the challenges SOs face is to explain complex and abstract security issues in a way that people without the expertise can understand. Consider spear phishing as an example. How would you explain that to someone who doesn't know what it is? What examples would you use? Which words, taxonomy and context would you use?

Most of us will focus on the terminology we know and use every day, without regard to the other person's level of knowledge.

The same is true for the other areas of expertise in the world: most people will use words, concepts and context they can relate to, and they will think that you understand that without even asking. Your challenge is that you are the one who must adapt to their needs: at no point can you assume that a person who does not work in security will understand what you are talking about. Hiding behind the terminology of your industry only works against you by alienating your audience.

To help others understand your message, you can change the wording and use concepts and terminology they relate to and understand. You may also try to convey the message in an entirely different way, as Mo Amin[28] puts it:

"Awareness demonstrated is awareness achieved."

For the preceding phishing example, you may set up a demonstration using equipment from your lab, and show in detail what is going on during an attack. Just remember to avoid the technical terms and instead focus on what is happening from a *business* point of view: a person clicks on the link and is taken to a hosted server that installs

---

[28] Mo Amin is a Certified Security Culture Coach and dedicates himself to building better security culture: _www.moamin.com_.

malware. Malware scans a computer for files of a particular type/name/date, and sends them to a different server.

This scenario is not very complicated to set up using a lab, and demonstrating the results can be done easily too: demonstrate that files of particular names/types are actually moved from the computer to the server without the person using the laptop knowing.

Just one word of warning: make sure you control the full environment, and let the person who is being taught use a lab computer, not their own.

This kind of demonstration does not require a large investment, and it can be done in a board meeting, in the hallway outside the lunchroom, in a coffee area or also virtually.

Similar demonstrations can show general malware, password strength, social media scraping and so much more. All it takes is a bit of planning.

Activities go better together. Combine a selection of three or more activities to have them support and strengthen the message you are creating. In our phishing example, you may consider presenting a series of short video lessons, an "Alert me" phone number to call if they suspect phishing, and perhaps a selection of stickers in addition to the phishing demonstrations.

It is important to remember that the activities you choose should be focused on the needs of the audience. Using your audience analysis in the Organisation module, you can determine the level of knowledge and interest of your target audience. Use that analysis to pick the kind of activities that will help your audience to understand and grow their competence.

The activities are closely tied to your goals, as defined in the Topics module, too. Activities should be designed and implemented to help you reach your goals. One question you can use to assess how your chosen activity will help you reach your goal, is:

"How will this activity help me reach my goal?"

Describing your answer is important to control your direction. It also makes sense to note your answer for later reference. The templates available at *securitycultureframework.com* will help you to select your activities, and to ensure your selection will in fact help you reach your goals.

Planner

The fourth part of the Security Culture Framework is the Planner. The Planner is a selection of different ways to plan and execute your security culture programme, where three elements are vital:

1. When to run activities.
2. When to do measurements (metrics).
3. When to revise and assess your progress.

The Planner is not another planning tool like Microsoft Project. Instead, it is a description of what actions a security culture programme should consist of, and at what interval. Templates are downloadable at *securitycultureframework.com.*

One example of a security culture campaign is the Security Culture Framework 12-week campaign. The 12-week campaign is one full iteration of a security culture programme, run over the course of 12 weeks. The campaign is divided into three parts, following the Planner module:

Four weeks of metrics, followed by six weeks of activities, and then two weeks of measuring progress, analysing results and revising future actions.

A 12-week campaign may look like this:

Week	Action	Comment
1	Set up team	Get the core security culture team
1	Define main goal	Set one main goal to work towards
1	Define subgoals	If desirable, define subgoals
2	Create baseline(s)	Using the goal metrics, collect data for baseline (as is)
2	Analyse	Use baseline data and defined goal state to create gap analysis
2	Select activities	Brainstorm a selection of activities to close the gap
3–4	Source activities	Create, develop or buy the preceding activities chosen
3	Plan activities	Plan when to execute each activity
5–10	Run activities	Activities do not have to be run at the same time!

11	Rerun baseline metric	Do the same measure as in week 2, collecting new data
11	Analyse	Use gap analysis: baseline vs. new metric = progress; new metric vs. goal = new gap
12	Revise	Consider your results. Consider what you would do differently. Revise accordingly

A note on the 12-week programme: this is a generic example, which you may have to change for your own needs. Some organisations need more time to run one iteration, and this is especially true in larger companies. You may have to adjust it to a six-month iteration, or even a 12-month cycle depending on your needs, your resources and the current culture.

The 12-week programme was designed as a bite-sized chunk. By creating a small, standardised approach, it becomes easy to set up and run security culture campaigns. This approach also helps you to keep your goals tangible, and to do small and efficient activities to build and maintain culture. Instead of a "Do it all" approach, the Security Culture Framework encourages you to take the small steps, each step building on the previous one, and steering you towards your overall goal of building and maintaining security culture.

Setting up your organisation to use the Security Culture Framework

With the basic knowledge of the Security Culture Framework, you are now ready to set up your organisation to use it to build and maintain security culture. You may use these steps to start.

- Set up your core security culture workgroup. Using the Organisation Module, set up your core team with one resource from the security office, one from HR and one from marketing or communications. If you do not have those resources internally, you may use external resources.

  In addition to your core team, you should create support for your security culture programme by getting your CEO to sponsor it. One way to get top-tier sponsorship is to set up a steering committee where you involve the key players, and get their support.

- Define goals and scope. Defining a long-term goal is a good idea early on, as it will help you steer your activities in one direction. A long-term goal may be defined using the SMART method mentioned earlier, or it may be described as a vision. The purpose of a long-term, overarching goal is to remind you of the direction you are directing your organisation towards, and to help you prioritise and select milestones and subgoals. Use this long-term goal to define your scope, resource requirements and long-term strategy.

- When you have defined a long-term goal, it is time to break it into bite-sized chunks, or 12-week campaigns. Start with your first campaign, and decide on one or a few goals you want to achieve.

- Define your target audience. Considering your goal, who will benefit most in your organisation? Are there some departments, locations or groups that stand out as more beneficial?

- Analyse your target audience. Who are they? How do they prefer to communicate? What is their security knowledge? Use the template available at *securitycultureframework.com* as well as the experience your marketing department have in analysing customer segments.

- Create baseline (as-is) measurement. Using your goal as a guiding light, decide how to measure your success, and create a baseline measurement to document your current status. Do a gap analysis to determine the difference between your baseline and your goal.

- Identify activities. Using your gap analysis, your defined goal(s) and your analysis of your target audience, you are ready to choose activities. Remember that learning activities come in a wide range – from classroom and e-learning sessions, to giveaways, posters and demos. Be creative, and allow yourself to try out different activities to see which gives the best results in any given setting and group. As long as you are confident that your activity is supporting your goal, you should be fine.

- Source activities. Now that you know what kinds of activities you want to use, it is time to either create them, buy them or download them. There are many suppliers of security trainings around, and approaching them with specific requirements of what you are looking for is a great way to help them supply you with exactly what you need. If you have in-house expertise, you may produce the content internally. If you do not have a budget, consider all the free sources of content available. For a growing list of suppliers, check out the *securitycultureframework.com* community.

- Plan and run activities. In your planner, add the different activities, their start, duration and end times, and any comments you find relevant. Then run the activities as you planned and watch as your organisation learns.

- Measure results. After the activities are successfully ran, it is time to do your second measurement. Using the same data source and method as you used to create your baseline metrics, collect the new status. If your activities were implemented successfully, you should notice differences between the baseline and the new metric. If you don't, there is no need to panic: there are a number of reasons why your data did not change:
  o they do not show what you try to measure
  o the changed behaviour you want to see takes longer to show
  o not enough data is available.

- Analyse results. Using the baseline data, your new data and your defined goals, analyse any progress you made, and try to understand why you get the results you get.

- Revise. While analysing your results, make notes of your findings. Consider what you could have done differently when it comes to activities, goals, timeframes and budgets, and put them in your report. For your next campaign, use your newfound knowledge to improve on what you did.

The first time you set up the Security Culture Framework in your organisation, it may require more time and resources. This is normal. Identifying the key resources for your core team may take some time, which you do not have to repeat every time you run a campaign – the team generally stays the same.

It is also normal that doing something new takes more focus than when you do something you are familiar with. The same is true with the Security Culture Framework. As you run a few campaigns, you start to get hold of the process, and soon you will notice how the framework is saving you and your organisation time and resources when building and maintaining security culture.

If you do find yourself in a squeeze and need help figuring out how to move forward, the community is only a browser away. You will find both certified Security Culture Coaches, certified Security Culture Practitioners and a growing number of users of the Security Culture Framework at *securitycultureframework.com*. And I did mention it is free and open, right?

CHAPTER 8: TIME IS ON YOUR SIDE

You have successfully reached the end of this book on security culture. You have learned what security culture is and how it relates to security awareness. You have tapped into social sciences with a focus on psychology, so we can better understand how people interact, behave and inform their actions. This is knowledge that is important to have when bringing about cultural change. You have also read about security culture metrics and how to use the Security Culture Framework to build and maintain security culture.

There are a few final things I need to share with you.

Reading this book does not make you an expert on this topic. Even writing this book, I do not consider myself the one know-it-all – there are so many different aspects of culture, people and behaviours that we still do not understand. That is one of the reasons I am back at the University of Oslo where I am reading psychology. I want to help the industry by building a body of knowledge on security culture. I am dedicating my time and resources because I believe it is important for us as an industry to understand people for real, if we want to bring about change.

However, reading this book shows that you, just like me, are interested in this topic. Hopefully that means you will bring about positive change in your organisation now and later. I also hope you find it interesting to learn more about culture, diversity, learning and communication. There is an abundance of topics related to security that is not directly to do with malware, firewalls and pen testing. These topics are not at all new. Since the dawn of human existence we have built security culture into our societies. I see no end to the need for understanding how we can become even better at this.

Changing culture takes time. Sometimes it works, other times it doesn't. Scientists disagree about the reasons and the methods. There are an unknown number of unknown factors that may or may not apply to your success. One thing is for sure, though: if you are not in charge of the culture yourself, culture will be in charge of you. Set your goals, and work towards them. Small steps does it.

My experience shows that a structured approach is more likely to yield success than any of the happy-go-lucky approaches I've seen. A programme that brings about change also plays with all elements of culture: technology, policies and people. Sometimes they succeed right away, and other times they need a number of tries.

What I see in the programmes we run is that time is an important asset. Have a long perspective. And by long, I mean 3-5 years' time. Longer if possible. Create a vision, or big goals for that period, and break it down into smaller targets you can use as milestones. Have at least one yearly target, and work to reach that one. Adjust your course as you learn more. And never settle down!

Building and maintaining culture is not something you do once and then you're done. It's an ongoing, never-ending process. Either you are in charge of it, or it controls you. Think of culture as a constant feedback loop creating a mutual change-cycle. You are part of the culture, part of that feedback loop, feeding it with your own behaviours, ideas and customs. The more of you who join forces and feed it with common behaviour, the more the culture will impact the others too. Use it to your benefits!

I welcome your insights, ideas and thoughts on the Security Culture Framework community at *securitycultureframework.com*. Let us join forces and build better security culture!

ITG RESOURCES

IT Governance Ltd sources, creates and delivers products and services to meet the real-world, evolving IT governance needs of today's organisations, directors, managers and practitioners.

The ITG website (*www.itgovernance.co.uk*) is the international one-stop-shop for corporate and IT governance information, advice, guidance, books, tools, training and consultancy.

Publishing Services

IT Governance Publishing (ITGP) is the world's leading IT-GRC publishing imprint that is wholly owned by IT Governance Ltd.

With books and tools covering all IT governance, risk and compliance frameworks, we are the publisher of choice for authors and distributors alike, producing unique and practical publications of the highest quality, in the latest formats available, which readers will find invaluable.

www.itgovernancepublishing.co.uk is the website dedicated to ITGP. Other titles published by ITGP that may be of interest include:

- CyberWar, CyberTerror, CyberCrime

  www.itgovernance.co.uk/shop/p-511-cyberwar-cyberterror-cybercrime-and-cyberactivism-second-edition.aspx

- Governance and Internal Controls for Cutting Edge IT

  www.itgovernance.co.uk/shop/p-1288-governance-and-internal-controls-for-cutting-edge-it.aspx.

- The Case for ISO27001: 2013

  www.itgovernance.co.uk/shop/p-1158-the-case-for-iso-27001-2013-second-edition.aspx

We also offer a range of off-the-shelf *toolkits* that give comprehensive, customisable documents to help users create the specific documentation they need to properly implement a management system or standard. Written by experienced practitioners and based on the latest best practice, ITGP toolkits can save months of work for organisations working towards compliance with a given standard.

To see the full range of toolkits available please see:

www.itgovernance.co.uk/shop/c-129-toolkits.aspx.

Books and tools published by IT Governance Publishing (ITGP) are available from all business booksellers and the following websites:

- *www.itgovernance.eu*
- *www.itgovernanceusa.com*
- *www.itgovernance.in*
- *www.itgovernancesa.co.za*
- *www.itgovernance.asia*

Training Services

Staff training is an essential component of the information security triad of people, processes and technology, and of building a security culture in an organisation. IT Governance's ISO27001 Learning Pathway provides information security courses from Foundation to Advanced level, with qualifications awarded by IBITGQ.

The ISO27001 Learning Pathway comprises the following courses:

- Foundation level
  - ○ ISO27001 Certified ISMS Foundation course
  - ○ ISO27001 Certified Internal Auditor course
  - ○ Information Security Foundation based on ISO27002 course.

- Advanced level
  - ○ ISO27001 Certified ISMS Lead Implementer Masterclass
  - ○ ISO 27001 Certified ISMS Lead Auditor course
  - ○ ISO27005 Certified ISMS Risk Management course
  - ○ ISO 27001:2013 ISMS Certified Transition course.

Many courses are available in Live Online as well as classroom formats, so delegates can learn and achieve essential career progression from the comfort of their own homes and offices.

Delegates passing the exams associated with out ISO27001 Learning Pathway will gain qualifications from IBITGQ, including CIS F, CIS IA, CIS LI, CIS LA, CIS RM and CIS 2013 UP).

IT Governance is an acknowledged leader in the world of ISO27001 and information security management training. Our practical, hands-on approach is delivered by experienced practitioners, who focus on improving your knowledge, developing your skills, and awarding relevant, industry-recognised certifications. Our fully integrated and structured learning paths accommodate delegates with various levels of knowledge, and our courses can be delivered in a variety of formats to suit all delegates.

For more information about IT Governance's ISO 27001 learning pathway, please see: *www.itgovernance.co.uk/ iso27001-information-security-training.aspx*.

For information on any of our many other courses, including PCI DSS compliance, business continuity, IT governance, service management and professional certification courses, please see: *www.itgovernance.co.uk/training.aspx*.

Professional Services and Consultancy

ISO27001, the international standard for information security management, sets out the requirements of an information security management system (ISMS), a holistic approach to information security that encompasses people, process, and technology. Only by using this approach to information security can organisations hope to instil an enterprise-wide culture of security.

Implementing, maintaining and continually improving an ISMS can, however, be a daunting task. Fortunately, IT Governance's consultants offer a comprehensive range of flexible, practical support packages to help organisations of any size, sector or location to implement an ISMS and achieve certification to ISO27001.

We have already helped more than 150 organisations to implement an ISMS, and with project support provided by our consultants, you can implement ISO27001 in your organisation.

At IT Governance we understand that information security is a business issue, not just an IT one. Our consultancy services assist organisations in properly managing their information technology strategies and achieving strategic goals. The benefits of choosing an IT Governance Consultancy Service are:

- We speak business, not technology: we are technology literate business consultants.
- We are vendor neutral, technology independent and framework agnostic, and tailor our consultancy to your organisation.
- Our transparent pricing enables you to control your costs.
- We have over ten years' consultancy experience.
- We have a proven track record, working with organisations worldwide.
- We help you increase internal buy-in to your project by using your resources.
- We focus on transferring knowledge and skill to the people within your organisation.

For more information on our ISO27001 consultancy service, please see: *www.itgovernance.co.uk/iso27001_consultancy.aspx*.

For general information about our other consultancy services, including for ISO20000, ISO22301, Cyber Essentials, the PCI DSS, Data Protection and more, please see: *www.itgovernance.co.uk/consulting.aspx*.

Newsletter

IT governance is one of the hottest topics in business today, not least because it is also the fastest moving.

You can stay up to date with the latest developments across the whole spectrum of IT governance subject matter, including; risk management, information security, ITIL and

IT service management, project governance, compliance and so much more, by subscribing to ITG's core publications and topic alert emails.

Simply visit our subscription centre and select your preferences:

www.itgovernance.co.uk/newsletter.aspx.

CPSIA information can be obtained at www.ICGtesting.com
Printed in the USA
BVOW06s1949291115

428780BV00009B/52/P